In Memory of
Richard Prince

LEGION

WW II Veteran

ARMS
& ARMOUR

ARMS
& ARMOUR

FREDERICK WILKINSON

CHANCELLOR
PRESS

To Jo

Acknowledgments

The illustration on page 67 is reproduced by courtesy of the Archbishop of Canterbury and the Trustees of Lambeth Palace Library. The illustrations on pages 61 bottom, 76 bottom, 84 right, 97 top and 108 top are reproduced by permission of the Trustees of the Wallace Collection.

Photographs
Graphische Sammlung Albertina, Vienna 79 top; Antikvarisk Topografiska Arkivet, Stockholm 44 top, 51 top; Archives Photographiques, Paris 39 top right; Ashmolean Museum, Oxford 19 left, 32 bottom; Australian War Memorial, Canberra 124 top; Bavaria Verlag, Gauting 43 left; Bibliothèque Nationale, Paris 58 left, 70; City of Birmingham Museum and Art Gallery, Birmingham 110 centre; Jean Bottin, Paris 37; British Library, London 57 bottom, 59, 136 top; British Museum, London 23, 34, 36, 46 bottom, 53 right, 68 top, 81 right, 146, 147 right; Central Office of Information, London 133; Chandler-Pohrt Collection, Great Lakes Indian Museum, Cross Village, Michigan 152 left, 152 right; Chester Beatty Library, Dublin 138 bottom; Christie, Manson and Woods, London 109 top; Crown copyright – reproduced with permission of the Controller of Her Majesty's Stationery Office 72, 77 bottom, 84 left, 149 top left, 149 bottom left; Deutsches Archäologisches Institut, Athens 28 bottom; Werner Forman Archive, London 25, 41 bottom left, 46 top, 47, 49, 134, 135 right, 142 right, 143 top, 148 bottom, 149 right; Freer Gallery of Art, Washington D.C. 33 right; Thomas Gilcrease Institute of American History and Art, Tulsa, Oklahoma 111; Photographie Giraudon, Paris 19 right, 32 top, 38, 39 left, 53 left, 77 top, 79 bottom, 80 bottom; Gunshots, London 14 top, 15 bottom, 16 left, 16 right, 17 left, 17 top right, 17 bottom right, 18 left, 18 right, 20 left, 22 centre, 29 bottom, 30 bottom, 31 bottom, 39 bottom, 43 right, 45 bottom, 45 right, 55 left, 57 top, 66 left, 68 right, 69 top, 73 bottom, 74 top, 74 bottom, 75 top, 75 bottom, 81 left, 82 bottom, 86 top, 87 top, 88 top, 88 bottom, 89 top, 90 left, 91 left, 93 top, 93 bottom, 94 top, 94 bottom, 96, 98 top, 100, 102 centre, 103 bottom, 105 top, 105 bottom, 107 left, 109 bottom, 110 top, 110 bottom, 112, 115 top, 115 bottom, 116 top, 117 bottom, 118, 120, 121, 122 bottom, 125 top, 125 centre, 126 top, 126 bottom, 127 top, 128 top, 128 bottom, 129 top, 131 top, 132 top, 135 left, 137 left, 139 left, 141 top, 141 bottom, 142 left, 143 bottom, 144; Hamlyn Group Picture Library endpapers, 14 bottom, 29 top, 31 top, 33 left, 40 bottom, 48, 50, 52, 73 top, 85, 87 bottom, 99, 102 top, 102 bottom, 106 top, 107 right, 108 bottom, 113 top, 114 left, 119 top, 136 bottom, 139 right, 150 left, 151 right; Hamlyn Group – Iain Reid 6–7; M. Hétier, Paris 44 bottom; Hans Hinz, Allschwil 11, 15 top; Hirmer Verlag, Munich 22 top, 22 bottom, 24, 30 top; M. Holford, Loughton 26, 28 top; Imperial War Museum, London 123, 124 bottom; A. N. Kennard 98 bottom; Kunsthistorisches Museum, Vienna 66 centre; Editions Robert Laffont, Paris 130; S. Guiley-Lagache, Paris 35 top; Lambeth Palace Library, London 67; Larousse, Paris 140 right; Bildarchiv Foto Marburg 21, 56 top; Metropolitan Museum of Art, New York 98 centre; Musée de l'Homme, Paris 12 right; Musée des Antiquités Nationales, Saint Germain-en-Laye 12 left; Musées Nationaux, Paris 83, 103 top, 150 right; Museum für Völkerkunde, Vienna 151 left; Museum of London 45 top; National Army Museum, London 89 bottom, 101 centre, 113 bottom, 114 right, 116 bottom; National Gallery, London 76 top; W. Keith Neal 106 top; Nederlands Lager- en Wapenmuseum, Leiden 80 top; New York Public Library 137 right; High Commission of New Zealand, London 147 top; Pierpont Morgan Library, New York 55 right, 56 bottom; Jean Roubier, Paris 61 top; Royal Small Arms Factory, Enfield 125 bottom; Seattle Art Museum, Seattle, Washington 148 top; Sheffield City Museum 41 top; Smithsonian Institution, Freer Gallery of Art, Washington D.C. 33 right; Sotheby Parke Bernet, London 140 left; Staatliche Museen zu Berlin 20 right; Stiftsarchiv, St Gallen 41 bottom right; U.S. Army 129 bottom; Victoria and Albert Museum, London 58 right, 66 right, 90 right, 92; Wallace Collection, London 61 bottom, 76 bottom, 84 right, 97 top, 108 top; Weidenfeld and Nicolson, London 40 top, 62, 63, 64, 65 top, 71, 82 top, 91 right, 95; Winchester Gun Museum, New Haven, Connecticut 117 top.

First published in 1978 by Hamlyn
This edition published in 1996 by Chancellor Press,
an imprint of Reed Consumer Books Limited
Michelin House, 81 Fulham Road
London SW3 6RB

© Reed International Books, 1978

ISBN 1 85152 957 8

Drawings by Terry Allen Designs Ltd. - Roger Courthold.

Produced by Mandarin Offset
Printed in China

Contents

Foreword

Weapons are almost as old as man himself. Since earliest time he has used them in the struggle to survive: to hunt for food and to protect himself from his enemy. As his technology advanced, so did his skill as a weapon maker, and today, throughout the whole world, he probably devotes more time, money and effort to his armaments than to anything else.

The main object of a weapon is at least to dissuade an attacker, at worst to kill him. Their purpose is unpleasant, but this does not mean that weapons are without interest or unattractive as art objects.

This book seeks to tell the story of the smaller, personal, hand weapons; the larger 'team' weapons such as artillery, aircraft, tanks, battle ships and submarines are not included. The range of material covered is enormous for weapons have been made in every shape and form. Some have been ingenious, some have been ridiculous, many have been effective and a few have been more lethal to the user than to the victim.

As each weapon was developed so the search for a counter-measure was started. The history of arms and armour is one of continual struggle between the weapon maker and the armourer; as soon as the former produces an effective weapon the latter comes up with a superior defence. Today the sword has been relegated to the parade and armour means lumbering tanks.

Without in any way denying the unpleasant nature of weapons there is still a fascinating story to be told in the development and history of these objects which have played such a large part in man's history.

The First Weapons

From the earliest times until well into the nineteenth century man had only three or four basic materials with which to construct his weapons for war or the chase.

In his evolutionary stages, it is probable that he made use of materials that were ready to hand, such as bone, wood and stone, simply picking up an odd piece that he came across and using it to hurl at or hit an enemy. One of the factors that distinguishes man from other primates is his skill as a tool-maker and later on he managed to fashion weapons in a particular shape to suit his own purposes out of raw material. He managed with weapons mainly of stone for several thousand years; he later learnt to fashion raw materials into other substances that were better suited to his ends, and he made compounds of bronze and iron. When the first civilizations emerged they did so alongside a developing technology which gave man harder, better weapons which he could use for organized warfare.

When and how the first weapon was used is not known, but it seems fairly certain that at least a million years ago man had discovered the use of stones as a convenient, ready to hand, form of tool. Some of the earliest stone tools and weapons are known as eoliths, literally 'dawn stones'. It seems likely that these owe their shape to the chance banging and rolling by wind and wave, and were not man-made.

A further step was made in the evolution of weapons when man discovered that whilst any rock would make a useful missile or hand weapon, one particular kind of stone was especially useful: flint. Flint is found distributed over most of the world's surface, and appears as lumps or nodules which are often covered with a layer of varying thickness known as the

Cave paintings have been discovered in Lascaux, France, which date as far back as 15,000 to 10,000 BC. This scene is thought to represent a wounded bison which has been pierced by a spear, and is possible evidence of man's earliest weapons.

patina, which is a coat of white silica. It may be that its strange appearance with its varying colours and sizes, or even its very commonness, attracted man to experiment with it. At some time, somewhere, he discovered a piece of flint that had been naturally shattered. He found that the edge of the flake was extremely sharp. With a stroke of genius, he connected the two

This cave painting from Teruel, Spain shows hunters armed with bows and arrows, although it is impossible to say what type of bow is used.

Flint of the Neolithic period carefully shaped with a very sharp point and edges. It could be mounted in a handle or bound to a shaft.
Musée des Antiquités Nationales, Saint Germain-en-Laye.

facts, and realized that the sharp piece of stone came from the large piece. Thus somewhere man banged two stones together and produced the first real flint tools.

The first of these flint tools of the Paleolithic, or Old Stone Age, are fairly crude and most are of the type known as hand-axes or biface. They are pear-shaped and were produced by hammering flints together and carefully paring away the outside until a pointed edge was produced. The primary use of these hand-axes was for chopping; they were however also used for other purposes. The point was probably used to pierce wood or skins and the edges could be used as a scraper to clean skins. When one of these hand-axes was mounted in a wooden handle, and used as an axe or as a club, man had produced his first weapon. 45,000 years ago, chiefly in areas around the Mediterranean, the crude, pear-shaped hand-axe was gradually refined and worked until it became smoother and better shaped. It was made in the shape of a wedge or chisel and a far sharper edge was given to it so that it could be used as a general multipurpose tool or weapon.

Another important discovery that primitive man made was that the pieces chipped off in the production of the axe had a use in their own right: they had a very sharp edge which could itself be shaped. (He also found that he could produce these flakes not only by striking them off but also by applying pressure at certain points on the nodules.) The smaller pieces he shaped to produce knives and scrapers but one extremely important new step was to use them in conjunction with the bow.

The bow was man's first complex long-range weapon. It effectively increased man's reach giving him the ability to strike at his prey or enemy from a considerable distance. The date of its first use will never be known but some indication can be deduced from the famous cave paintings at Lascaux which date from about 25,000 BC: some of the animals are shown with a missile embedded in them which appear to have vanes fitted, suggesting an arrow or some form of vaned spear. Remains of pine wood staves that were almost certainly bows have been found of around the same date, and in eastern Spain a cave painting dating from the Mesolithic (or Middle) Stone Age clearly shows a bow being used. In this painting a group of men are attacking a deer and the painter draws two different bows. Whether this means that two forms of bow were used or whether the artist simply varied his style, is impossible to say. One is a D-shaped or segment bow common among modern pre-industrial societies, the other is of the double convex type, with a short, central section which is straight and a curved section at each end. Remnants of prehistoric bows discovered in Switzerland are mainly

of yew, and it is interesting to note that thousands of years later the English bowman still preferred yew as the best material for his bow. Surviving evidence seems to suggest that most of these primitive bows were fairly long, probably up to 6 feet. Some bows discovered in Denmark have a flat cross-section while others are D-shaped, the flat side facing the archer when in use.

It is likely that the first arrows were little more than just a straight reed. If they were made of wood, then the tip may have been hardened by being charred in a fire, and certainly spears with fire hardened points have been excavated. Another discovery made by early man was that the penetration of the arrow could be greatly increased if a small piece of flint was fixed to the tip. At first any suitably shaped piece was used, but gradually a whole arrow technology evolved and the very large number of surviving examples suggests that production rates were high.

Surviving arrowheads from the Stone Age can be grouped into five main types, according to certain distinguishing features. The earliest heads were relatively unsophisticated, and were triangular, leaf- and lozenge-shaped. In the second and third millennium BC the tanged

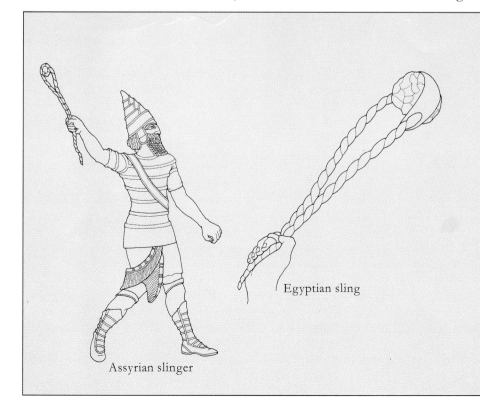

Assyrian slinger

Egyptian sling

THE SLING
The sling is one of man's earliest long range weapons, and has been used from the earliest times, either held in the hand or mounted on a staff. The stones used as missiles were usually smooth pebbles, but often they were specially shaped stones.

One sling found in an Egyptian tomb dating from 800 BC was 22 inches long and was of plaited cord with a loop at one end through which the first finger was slipped. A stone was placed in the centre pouch and the other end of the cord was held in the hand. When the stone was to be cast the end held in the hand was released; with practice, a very accurate throw could be made.

Notable users of the sling were the hoplite soldiers of Ancient Greece, and also people from the Pacific Islands who plaited them from grass or human hair.

arrowhead developed. This had a small neck projecting back from the point, which let into a slit cut at the end of the arrow. It was held in place by some naturally occurring adhesive such as resin or, more likely, by thonging that was carefully tied round the neck of the arrow. The barbed arrowhead, which was almost certainly one of the last to be developed, does not appear until about 2000 BC. Whether early man ever developed his arrow technology to the point where different shapes were produced for hunting and war, is not clear. It is of interest to note that experiments comparing the penetrative powers of steel and flint heads have shown that, surprisingly, flint can give a better penetration.

Although flint was the most commonly used naturally occurring material for weapon production it was not the only one, and all over the world is found evidence of the use of animal horns and the stings of some fish. In South and Central America another mineral, known as obsidian, was used to give a particularly nasty cutting edge to a club.

Flint can be fashioned and shaped but it has one basic and inherent weakness: like many very hard substances it has low impact strength. If a large piece receives a sharp blow it shatters, which means that it is virtually impossible to produce an effective sword or dagger from flint. Flint swords have been excavated in some places (Denmark for example) but it is extremely unlikely that they were ever intended as weapons or had more than a ceremonial significance. This being the case man could only develop his flint technology to

a certain point. The solution to this problem was found at some indeterminate date somewhere in the Middle East, where small pins of copper, some of man's earliest metalwork, have been found which have been dated by radio carbon method to somewhere around 5000 BC. Early man may well have known of copper long before he discovered the secret of working it. Naturally occurring copper is found as tiny pieces or as rather diffuse, spongy chunks which may weigh as much as several hundredweight. It can be shaped by hammering for it is reasonably malleable but when hammered it becomes very brittle and easily cracks. Early smiths soon found this but at some time the copper was, by accident or design, heated and allowed to cool: in other words it was annealed. If this hammering and annealing is repeated it is possible to produce quite a hard edge.

Once man had learnt how to cast metal, he could manufacture on a larger scale a large number of

Top left:
Left: Bronze arrowhead with long tang to secure it to the shaft.
Right: Blade of bronze dagger with rivets at the top of the blade where the hilt was secured. Persian *c.* 1800 BC.

Top right:
Top: Flat, bronze spearhead.
Middle: Axehead with a socket and loop for fixing it to a shaft.
Bottom: Ornate axehead from Luristan.

different weapons. Initially, the smiths naturally sought to copy the old flint axeheads in the new material: the copper axes were cast in open moulds which were probably flat stones with the shape for the axe rubbed or chipped out ready for the metal to be poured in and left to set. The earliest samples found are simple, flat axes weighing about 4 ounces, and examples of stone moulds have been found in Ireland. A few of these axeheads are very big, over $12\frac{1}{2}$ inches long and weighing some 6 pounds.

How long the smith worked only with pure copper is not known but at some point his skill and knowledge advanced to a stage where he realized that this crude metal could be improved by the addition of other components. Either by accident or design some tin was mixed with the copper and the first bronze ingot was cast. The proportion of copper to tin varies enormously but a normal proportion is on average, 10% tin to 90% copper. Bronze also contains a small percentage of other chemicals such as

arsenic which affect its texture, making it harder. Lead is another mineral which was later added, probably to make the molten metal flow more easily. It has also been suggested that it may merely have been put in as a makeweight; perhaps sharp practice by the smith!

The Bronze Age began somewhere around 1500 BC although it is difficult to be precise and the compound remained the chief weapon material until around 750 BC. Over the intervening centuries the smith's skill and mastery of the material increased. His first rather crude castings became more complex and advanced until the late examples indicate a mastery of the considerable skills involved in casting swords, daggers, spearheads and axes. Generally bronze daggers are fairly simple and the hilts were fitted with grips of bone or wood, perhaps bound on with leather or with a bronze rivet driven through them. For the nobles of a tribe or community the hilts were often embellished with precious metal or ivory.

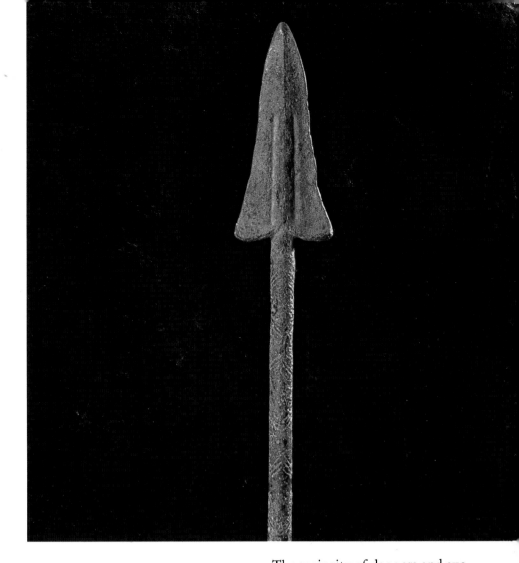

Right:
Bronze lance or spear head from Luristan (Iran). It has some simple incised decoration. *c.* 1500 BC. Length of head and shaft 12¾ inches (32.4 cm).

Below:
Bronze sword blade of early type with rivets which held the hilt in position. The shape indicates that it was primarily a thrusting weapon. *The Museum of London.*

Bottom right:
Bronze axehead from Luristan finely cast and of a type commonly found in this area and date. (2nd millenium BC.) *Iran Bastan Museum, Teheran.*

The majority of daggers and axe-heads, some of which are quite complex with loops for the attachment of shafts or with sockets to hold the haft, were usually cast in two-piece moulds. These were probably cut from stone but clay moulds were also used and some of the stone moulds have cavities which were filled with clay in order to be able to produce a particular shape. A clay mould was made from a wooden former, carefully shaped and smoothed, which was pressed into the damp clay to leave an impression. As the smiths' skill developed they were able to tackle the more complex task of producing sword and hilt in one piece.

Around the Mediterranean, by about 1500 BC, the dagger was developed to become more like a sword. The blade was now 2 or 3 feet long and often not more than half an inch wide. It seems that at first the blade and hilt were cast separately and then riveted together. This construction meant that there was an inherent weakness at this point – as many a warrior

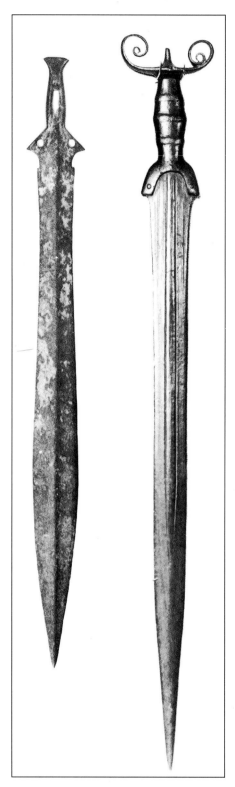

Left: Bronze Age sword of the typical leaf shape, although this example is rather broader than usual. The hilt would have had plates of bone or wood on each side. Overall length 24½ inches (62.2 cm). *The Museum of London.*
Right: Typical Bronze Age sword with large curving horns or antennae on the pommel. These swords were apparently popular in north Europe and date from 1100 to 650 BC. This one was found in Denmark.
British Museum, London.

Left: Bronze Age sword found in Ireland. The blade had been broken near the hilt and repaired. 26 inches (66 cm).
Right: Bronze Age dagger from Luristan, without the grips. 15½ inches (39.4 cm).
Both weapons date from around 2000 BC.

must have discovered when he was left with the grip in his hand and the blade on the ground. If the weapon was used primarily for stabbing the danger was less but the number of excavated blades with the rivets wrenched sideways is sufficient to suggest that this nice point was forgotten.

Some time around 1000 BC the characteristic sword of the Bronze Age appeared. This was leaf-shaped with the blade and hilt cast in one piece. The tang, which is the extension to hold the grip, widened at the top of the blade, which narrowed at first and then swelled out again towards the point. Now that the weakness at the hilt had been eliminated, the swords could be used to stab or slash. The tang would have been covered with shaped plates of bone or wood and again bound with leather.

However efficient the Bronze Age craftsman became, he could not, except within narrow limits, control the characteristics of his material. Bronze made an efficient weapon, but not as hard a one as a warrior would wish. It could be sharpened but the keen edge would be lost quite quickly and the need for constant resharpening would have been a handicap. What the warrior wanted was a harder, more durable metal, one capable of being worked but of sufficient hardness to retain an edge.

Such a material was to hand in the form of meteorites, and to early man it must have appeared to be a gift direct from the gods! It is not difficult to fashion meteoric iron into knife blades or tools, but the supply of meteoric iron was very limited. It was probably the tribe known as the Hittites, who came originally from Asia Minor, who first discovered the secret of extracting iron from native ores and fashioning it into a tool or weapon. They seem to have guarded their knowledge well for archaeological evidence suggests that they possessed iron swords and daggers long before other people in the same area. Perhaps because of their new 'secret' weapon the Hittites became supreme in their area and ruled an empire; it was only when they lost their supremacy and began to decline from around 1280 BC that iron technology began to spread across the Near East, reaching Europe around 1200 BC. From Europe the craft was brought to Britain by the so-called Hallstatt people about 500–400 BC.

Iron has one great virtue in that it is much harder than bronze but its use introduced several new problems. It was a far more difficult material to work with and the furnace construction needed for its production is more involved. For the archaeologist and historian one great drawback of iron is that, combined with water, it produces rust. The quantity of surviving evidence is limited as wind and weather have reduced most of these early weapons to mouldering, blackened chunks of rusted metal, but enough blades have survived, many only because of the scabbard, for some conclusions to be drawn. Since the cutting edge was all important the scabbard was normally made of wood so that there would be no metal rubbing against the blade. Two thin strips of wood were shaped around the blade and then wrapped round with leather, strengthened perhaps with bands of metal and a metal tip known as the chape. Sometimes these scabbards were lined with sheepskin, the natural grease in the fleece helping to preserve the blades from rust.

Some Iron Age swords are made to the same pattern as those of the Bronze Age: it must be remembered that the two periods overlapped and the advent of iron did not mean that bronze was abandoned. In some cases swords have been discovered whose hilt is of bronze while the blade is of iron. One interesting aspect of sword manufacture of this period is the existence of so-called 'currency bars' which are long narrow bars of iron. It is suggested that they were partly finished sword blades and the assumption is that they were produced at a foundry and then bartered or sold to smiths who would fashion them into a sword. Most of the bars are about 30 inches long. They appear to have originated mainly in the south-west of England, around the Cotswolds.

Hilt of bronze sword with flat disc pommel. Found in central Europe. *Ashmolean Museum, Oxford.*

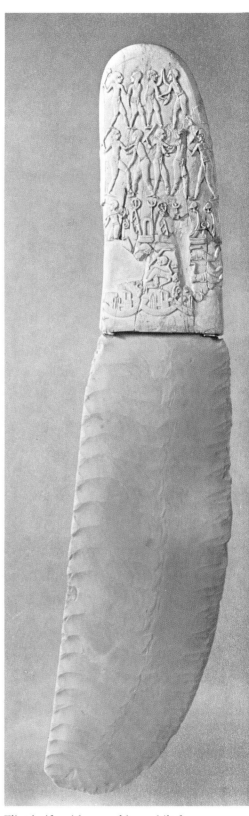

Flint knife with carved ivory hilt from Egypt, *c.* 3400 BC. Discovered at Gebel-El-Arak. *Musée du Louvre, Paris.*

This basalt block from Zincirli bears a carving of a Hittite warrior (c. 850 BC). He holds a shield which is a smaller version of the Greek figure of eight shield. He is armed with a sword and a spear.
Vorderasiatisches Museum, Berlin.

Corroded, excavated specimen of an Iron Age sword with the typical 'horn' pommel found on so many of these swords. *c.* 750 BC.
British Museum, London.

The majority of Iron Age swords have blades between 25 and 30 inches long although there are variations in pattern and design. Close metallurgic examination of the structure of these swords indicates that they were fashioned by one of two methods. One was to shape the blade and, when cold, hammer the edge, a process which gives a much harder finish. The other way was to have the blade built up of several layers of metal. The iron sword seems to have been primarily a slashing rather than a thrusting sword for many lack a real point. The hilt was often fitted with two long horns as were some of the Bronze Age weapons and these appear around 600 BC.

Thus by 400 BC the weapon makers had at their disposal the use of flint, bronze and iron which might, in some areas, be supplemented by natural materials such as horn, wood and hides. Differing cultures and civilizations took these materials and developed them producing weapons and armour which were often similar but differed in detail As one culture impinged on another so there was an interaction and styles of armour, weapons, tactics and strategy were constantly changing and developing.

The Ancient World

When man learned to use metal for the manufacture of his weapons, he had made a major technological discovery. He could now produce a large number of weapons with a wide variety of edges for stabbing or cutting – and he could also produce them on a large scale. The discovery of copper and bronze was one of the many factors that facilitated the growth of settled urban communities, and of the first civilizations.

Two of the first main civilized communities settled in two areas in the Middle East: the Nile Valley, and in Mesopotamia (modern Turkey and Iraq) along the fertile banks of the Tigris and the Euphrates. These communities were to develop into the civilizations of Ancient Egypt and Sumeria, both of which were to make considerable use of metal technology for their armaments. Ancient Egyptian technology had developed to such a point by the second millennium BC that its craftsmen could produce a sword with blade and hilt cast in one piece: this was the *khopesh* which was peculiar to Egypt and had a very sharply-curved, sickle-like blade. It is conceivable that the hilt was long enough to permit a two-handed grip, which would have meant that the weapon had considerable cutting power. The Egyptians also used clubs with heads of shaped stone as well as large axes with a curved blade secured to a wooden shaft. In Mesopotamia, splendid ceremonial daggers

A detail from a chest from the tomb of Tutankhamun showing Nubian warriors with their small, oval shields, which are all decorated with patterns. *Egyptian Museum, Cairo.*

Top left:
Superbly fashioned in gold, this parade helmet of Meskalam-Dug was found in the grave of a rich nobleman of Ur. It was made from a single sheet of 15-carat gold. The holes around the edge were for a padded lining.
Iraq Museum, Baghdad.

Centre left:
The Egyptian chariot speeds along as the Pharaoh, Seti I (1309–1291 BC), stands holding his bow and brandishing a *khopesh* above his head.
British Museum, London.

Bottom left:
This chest from the tomb of Tutankhamun is of wood with painted stucco decoration. It shows the king at war and the hunt; in this picture he stands in his chariot discharging arrows at his enemies.
Egyptian Museum, Cairo.

Opposite:
The Standard of Ur. The mosaic decoration on this box-like object shows scenes from war with chariots, prisoners and, at the centre, troops with some form of helmet and thick cape which may have been made of felt with some extra plates for protection.
(*c.* 2700 BC.)
British Museum, London.

have been found in royal Sumerian tombs, some made of gold with hilts inlaid with precious stones. Some centuries later in the same region, the Assyrians had swords placed in scabbards which were sometimes decorated with curling tips on the mouth and the chape.

It is a feature of the history of arms and armour that there is a constant struggle between the armourer and the weapon maker to produce better equipment: when the weapon maker adds to the warrior's armoury the armourer develops a countermeasure. When the first man struck a blow with a stick the victim defended himself either by counter-attacking or by some sort of defence. If he used another stick to ward off the blow, then the first shield had been invented. By the time he had at his disposal materials which could be worked into a great variety of shapes and sizes, the need for some purpose-made protection was obviously greater. The first positive evidence for the shield is not found until the emergence of Egyptian civilization, in two paintings that date back to 4000 BC. From these

it would seem that the first shields were simply tough animal skins, perhaps used in several layers on a wooden base. No doubt thick hides, such as those from the skins of rhinoceroses, elephants or crocodiles were used whenever possible.

The Egyptians did not develop body armour to any appreciable degree: their troops continued to be protected, according to the paintings, with little more than a shield. By 1900 BC this was generally smaller, and was decorated over the whole of its surface with various patterns. Even when the New Kingdom was founded around 1560 BC, it seems very unlikely that body armour was used by Egyptian troops; shields of this time were on the whole even smaller and roughly rectangular in shape. The first reliable evidence that would show how the shields were constructed came when Tutankhamen's tomb, which dates from about 1350 BC, was discovered. The king's shields were of wood covered with antelope skin, and this form of construction is confirmed by a wall painting of the 13th century BC which shows a shield maker stretching these skins in place over the wooden shield.

Helmets also seem to be noticeably lacking from the armoury of the Egyptians although some of their wall paintings do show troops carrying a long, pointed sword and a small, round shield, and wearing a horned helmet. It has been suggested that these were mercenaries employed by the Egyptians. It is during the period of roughly 1500 to 1200 BC that there is evidence of a more extensive use of scale armour.

Scale armour is a form of construction whereby metal plates are either stitched, riveted or tied to a garment. It is a simple, if tedious, way of constructing armour; the metal-working skill required is minimal since only small plates need to be forged and drilled. It seems likely that it was used all over the Middle East and there is written evidence from the reign of Tuthmosis III (c. 1440 BC) who boasts of how he captured 200 sets of scale armour. In a painting from the time of Tuthmosis IV (c. 1415 BC) a driver of a chariot is shown wearing a coat of scale armour. One problem with this type of armour is that it is difficult to cover the body completely. Certain parts of the body such as the armpit are difficult to cover with small metal plates. It is of interest to note that in the painting of Tuthmosis IV the chariot driver is shown with an arrow piercing him at this very vulnerable spot. From this period scale armour is increasingly depicted on wall paintings and carvings. Archaeological samples from Egypt vary in size from about $2\frac{1}{2}$ inches by $1\frac{1}{2}$ inches to $4\frac{3}{4}$ inches by $2\frac{1}{2}$ inches and are only about $\frac{1}{10}$ inch thick. Another drawback of scale armour is the number of plates needed to cover the body. Contemporary accounts give figures ranging from 680 to well over a thousand.

Further to the east, in Mesopotamia, the more warlike Sumerians introduced an important new military concept. Their spearmen were trained to advance in close-packed groups so that the spears gave the appearance of a vast hedgehog. This formation, the phalanx, was well established by the third millenium BC for it is depicted on a relief of this date called the Stele of Vultures. The tremendous impetus of such a formation would make it extremely difficult to stop but it was vital to keep the men in their close-packed formation. They obviously needed some protection and the phalanx men had large shields which protected the whole of the body from shoulder to ankle. Carvings indicate that the spear was held in both hands so the shield must, presumably, have had some kind of strap which hung around the neck so leaving the hands free. One puzzling feature of these

A phalanx from the Stele of Vultures (*c.* 2500 BC). The troops are secure behind their large shields and only their spears protrude. Their helmets are of particular interest since they are one of the earliest examples of armour, although whether they are made of leather or metal is not clear.
Musée du Louvre, Paris.

shields is a series of circles very clearly depicted on the front. It may well be that the increased supply of bronze permitted these shields to be strengthened with rondels in much the same way as on later shields.

Another interesting feature shown by the Stele of Vultures is that the troops are depicted wearing helmets. Although no conclusion can be drawn as to the material, it is unlikely that they were all of bronze and they may conceivably have been fashioned of treated leather. The fairly close-fitting helmets are conical with a neck-guard extending down almost to the shoulders. They appear to have a face bar, known as a nasal, rather like those found on the later Norman helmets, which would have given some protection against a sword cut.

A shield may be an efficient means of defence but it is also a cumbersome one, for it requires the use of either one or both hands; it can be awkward to manoeuvre and it restricts quick and easy movement. It seems likely from the available evidence that body armour was first used as an alternative means of defence by the Sumerians some time during the second millenium BC. Carvings show the soldiers with a cape reaching from the shoulder down to the ankle and since they carry no shields it is reasonable to suppose that the cape had replaced the shield. The surface of these capes is marked with a series of rings, rather like the earlier shields, and this suggests a reinforced defence. Perhaps the cape was of leather or other material to which were fastened plates of copper or bronze – it is unlikely to have been iron at this period. A cape such as this would leave the hands free to manage a spear or a bow while still offering some protection. These same troops are often shown with helmets and it has been suggested that they represent the heavy infantry who were intended to take the brunt of the attack.

By about 1000 BC the Assyrian civilization was in control and their sculpture glorifies their campaigns and victories. Their bowmen also made use of scale armour in the form of short-sleeved coats which reached only to their knees; they also wear helmets. Since the bow needs both hands the archer could not possibly hold a shield. The Assyrian archers are shown with a second man whose sole job it was to carry a shield to protect the bowman. The sculptures would suggest that the shield was made of plaited reeds. Later these shield carriers were replaced by large shields which the archer could move into position in the same way as the pavise was used in the Middle Ages.

The foot soldiers of the Assyrian army were mostly spearmen who carried a circular or rectangular shield and wore a metal helmet with a small crest. Assyrian cavalry were protected in much the same way although their helmets are shown without crests.

Around 1500 BC a new culture was emerging further to the west in the Mediterranean. A migratory people known as the Achaeans had spread south and eventually occupied the country that came to be known as Greece. The Achaeans ruled the city of Mycenae, which around the middle to late Bronze Age was one of the main centres of civilization. Ancient writers such as the poet Homer tell us a great deal about Greek warfare, and archaeologists have been able to confirm some of the details. For example, Homer refers to the use of a 'boar's tusk' helmet and for some time this was not understood. One archaeologist came across a number of boar's tusks at Mycenae which were slightly curved, and with a flash of genius he realized that by cutting them in half longitudinally and carefully arranging them it would be possible to cover the surface of a helmet to form a light but efficient head defence. His brilliant deduction was confirmed by some carvings found at Mycenae which show helmets with rows of

King Ashurbanipal (668–626 BC) is here shown hunting on horseback and drawing back his short bow.
British Museum, London.

Assyrian archers and spearmen all wearing conical helmets with earflaps. Their armour is of lamellar form and made up of a large number of small plates.
British Museum, London.

crescent shapes facing alternate directions. This style of helmet seems to have continued in use for several centuries.

The Mycenaean warrior's main defence was the shield and those found at Mycenae seem to have been particularly large. They were probably made of oxhide for they are shown in paintings with patches of dark colouring of exactly the shape and spacing as would appear on a hide stretched over a wooden frame. The commonest shape is one that was also used by the Hittites: the 'violin' shaped shield which is circular but with the centre pinched in. This would curve round the body and so give maximum protection. The other type is rectangular although the top section, instead of being flat, is curved. These shields would almost certainly have had at least two straps with which they would have been attached to one arm, and probably a third, longer strap to enable the warrior to hang it round the neck when in action or

sling it over his back when on the march.

Although scale armour was widely used throughout the eastern Mediterranean, armour fashioned from larger, single plates is far rarer although there is evidence of its use. One set found in the grave of a warrior at Dendra, near Mycenae, and dated to around the fifteenth century BC, is a remarkable piece of work. It consists of a tubular defence for the body with some plates hanging down from the lower section to protect the thighs. There is a throat-guard which is somewhat crude in shape but of a reasonable design, two large shoulder-guards and plates (known as greaves) for the lower leg. The weight must have been considerable and although maximum protection was given the inconvenience was probably also enormous. This may have been the reason for its comparatively limited use for it does not seem to have survived much beyond the fifteenth century BC. Greek paintings from this period seem to suggest, although this is questioned by some authorities, that the main body armour was fashioned from material: in other words, it was soft armour which was occasionally strengthened by scale plates.

However, from about 1200 BC when Mycenae seems, owing to an invasion of a new people, the Dorians, to have virtually disappeared from the stage of power, there is very little archaeological evidence of great use of body armour and the inference is that most of the armour used was of the soft material type. Excavations have produced fragments of folded linen which could well be the soft armour referred to in poetry since padding would dull the blow of a mace and could even deflect or muffle the cut of a sword.

Around the eighth century BC, there begins what is known as the Classical age of Greek civilization, based chiefly on the city states of Athens, Sparta, Thebes, Argos, Corinth and Mycenae, each of which possessed a well equipped and efficient army. Certainly, from about 800 BC the Greek paintings begin to show greater use of helmets

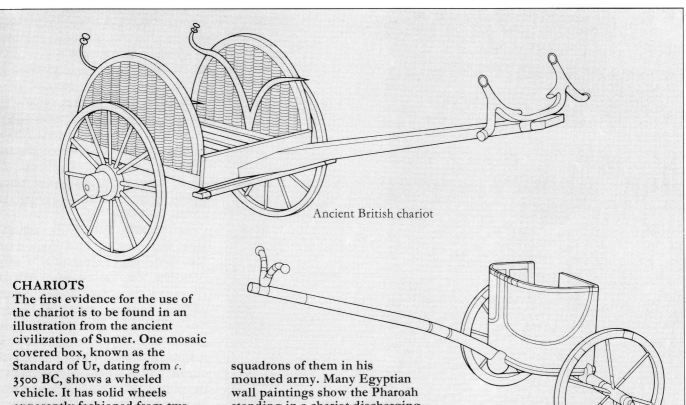

Ancient British chariot

Egyptian chariot

CHARIOTS

The first evidence for the use of the chariot is to be found in an illustration from the ancient civilization of Sumer. One mosaic covered box, known as the Standard of Ur, dating from *c.* 3500 BC, shows a wheeled vehicle. It has solid wheels apparently fashioned from two half discs and is pulled by two asses, so it was, presumably, not very fast. The chariot held a driver and a warrior who threw javelins which were carried in a quiver mounted on the high front.

Faster vehicles were developed in Asia Minor early in the second millenium BC. These reduced the overall weight by using spoked instead of solid wheels and were pulled by horses rather than asses, which obviously meant that they could move much faster. The Hyksos, a mysterious race from the Middle East, were masters of chariot warfare and conquered the powerful Egyptians *c.* 1750 BC. When Egypt finally threw them out *c.* 1580 BC the chariots formed an important part of the Egyptian army – Amen Hotep I, *c.* 1550, is recorded as having whole

squadrons of them in his mounted army. Many Egyptian wall paintings show the Pharoah standing in a chariot discharging his arrows.

Later, around 1100 BC the Assyrians used a larger chariot which held three men: a driver, a spear thrower or archer and a shield bearer to protect the other two.

By 1500 BC chariots were in use on the mainland of Greece and, judging by contemporary illustrations, they were very similar to the Egyptian form with spoked wheels, a high front and a single shaft with a yoke-like collar for the horses. The body was very simple with little more than a rail and floor for the riders.

The chariot was most effective in battle when used in large numbers to make massed charges at speed for their impetus could help smash their way through lines of spearmen.

The Ancient Britons made use of chariots and impressed their Roman enemies by running along the central shaft to strike at the foe and then back to the body of the chariot. All this was done whilst the chariot was moving at speed. It seems likely that these Celtic and British chariots had a more substantial body with a fenced-in back, front and sides. The axles were sometimes fitted with projecting blades, an idea possibly introduced by the Persians.

The chariot eventually fell out of favour as a weapon of war although they were retained as racing or ceremonial vehicles.

with the earliest ones being slightly conical with a crest on the top. The 'violin' shield seems to have been replaced by a round one and this is strengthened with a central bronze dome or boss. Bronze discs have also been excavated dating from around 600 BC which are pierced, suggesting that they formed sections. However, their circular shape means that they would have been unsuitable for scale armour as circles do not fit together as easily as squares or rectangles; they may have been intended for decorations

or for helmets.

Body armour and helmets were still being developed and from about 700 BC one form of helmet begins to appear more and more in the paintings. This is the Corinthian helmet which extended up from the shoulders and swept in a graceful curve to cover the head completely. There was an opening at the front to accommodate the nose and eyes and a bar or nasal that projected forward to give protection against the face being slashed. The whole helmet was hammered from a single

piece of bronze – a tremendous technical achievement – and was padded to reduce the effect of any blow that it stopped. Vision was rather limited as was hearing since the helmet covered the ear and the padding would further deaden any sound. It may well have been this problem of poor hearing that led to the introduction of the so-called Chalcidian helmet, which resembles the Corinthian but which is smaller with a less pronounced forward sweep to the cheek guards; most important however were the

27

two sections cut out on either side presumably to allow better hearing.

The Illyrian helmet which dates from the late seventh century BC is like the Corinthian but much simpler and much less technically difficult to produce: it was made in two halves and then joined together by a ridge that ran crosswise across the top. The helmet consisted of a skull with two triangular cheek pieces which almost reached the chest.

In the fifth century yet another style, the so-called Thracian helmet, was developed which was a cross between the Corinthian and the Illyrian. It had a high domed crown, a small peak which extended from ear to ear and protection to the face was given by two scalloped cheek pieces which resembled those of the Illyrian helmet but which were more elaborate in shape.

The last common type to be produced, the Boeotian helmet, was worn by cavalry largely because it did not impede hearing or reduce the range of vision. It consisted of a skull with a wide brim which drooped down and forwards so that the face was given some protection.

Up to the eighth century BC, Greek warfare had consisted mainly of single combat. Around this time, a new style of war was developed involving huge bodies of men. The Greek phalanx first appeared in the city state of Argos, and was composed of hoplites who took their name from the *hoplon*, a large round shield. The *hoplon* was roughly 3 feet in diameter and like earlier shields was fashioned of wood and bronze. Because this shield was comparatively heavy, a bronze arm loop was fitted on the back and a leather grip strap secured to the edge. The hoplite passed his left arm through the loop and gripped the strap.

A good idea of the hoplite in action is given by contemporary paintings and vases. His breast- and backplate were of bronze and were known as the cuirass, which had a collar which rose up above the chest and a very slightly flared waist. The head was protected by the style of helmet in fashion, usually the Corinthian, whilst the lower

part of the legs left uncovered by the shield were protected by bronze plates fitted to the shape of the leg and known as greaves. These do not appear to have had any straps and were presumably held in place by the actual springiness of the metal gripping against the padding. The corselet of bronze was normally plain but from about the fifth century BC it was often shaped to suggest the muscles of the body. There seem to have been occasions when extra protection was worn in the form of bands at the wrist, on the upper arm and occasionally on the thigh.

The hoplites' chief weapon was, of course, the iron-headed spear which was produced in a variety of shapes and sizes. The Mycenaeans spear was very large, the pole 10 feet in length and the head 2 feet. In some Mycenaean tombs spear-heads only 6 inches long have been found which probably came from light, throwing spears or

Top left:
These archers and slingers from Sennacherib's army are protected by a bearer who carries a shield probably fashioned from bundles of reeds. *British Museum, London.*

Bottom left:
Greek Corinthian helmet of bronze. It was shaped so that it could be worn over the head or pushed back on the forehead. *Deutches Archäologisches Institut, Athens.*

Top right:
A Greek vase, *c.* 530 BC, shows Achilles and Penthesilea, the Amazon warrior, in close combat. Both are armed with hoplons and spears. Achilles wears a crested Corinthian helmet and a bronze cuirass. Penthesilea has a leopard skin over her armour and has a somewhat unusual open-faced helmet. *British Museum, London.*

Bottom right:
A bronze, Chalcidian helmet showing the smaller neck guard and more open face. Found at Salonika. (5th century BC.) *British Museum, London.*

29

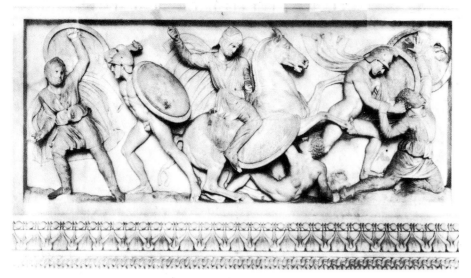

Left:
Carved panel from the Alexander sarcophagus (late 4th century BC), showing details of the hoplon, and also helmets with hinged cheek pieces.
Arkeoloji Müzerleri, Istanbul.

Below:
Attic painting on a clay mixing bowl from Cerveteri showing Achilles and Memnon in battle. They fight naked and their helmets are of the Corinthian style. (*c.* 490 BC.)
British Museum, London.

Opposite top:
Cast bronze figure of a Greek warrior wearing a Corinthian style helmet. It probably represents a hoplite riding into battle.
Found at Lucania (now Basilicata), Italy. 6th century BC.
British Museum, London.

Opposite bottom:
Based on excavated examples, this helmet and armour is a superb reconstruction of a Roman legionary's helmet and *lorica segmentata.*

javelins. The early Greeks seem to have fought with two or three spears some of which were light javelins. In the seventh century BC the hoplites are often shown with two spears but by the fifth century BC only a single spear was carried.

In addition to the spear, most hoplites carried, from about the sixth century BC, a sword known as a *kopis*, a name sometimes linked with the Egyptian *khopesh*. The kopis replaced an earlier, cruder sword which had a single, straight cross-guard, a thick hilt and a straight blade which swelled out towards the point making it a slashing rather than a stabbing weapon. The blade and hilt of the new *kopis* was fashioned in one piece and the hilt curved backwards in the shape of a letter C to form a simple guard. The gently curved blade was narrow at the grip, becoming wider part of the way along and then tapering to the point. In shape it resembled the modern Gurkha *kukri*. The inside edge of the curve was the sharp one and it was intended to be used with a down cutting sweep from behind the left shoulder. It was carried in a sheath hung from a baldric high up on the left hand side of the body. Should the spear be dropped or broken the sword was easily accessible and could be drawn quickly up over the top of the head and slashed downwards.

There were also some Greek soldiers that were armed with the sling, the javelin and the bow. The sling seems to have been the particular weapon of the people of Rhodes: it was made from dried gut or sinew with a small piece of leather secured in the middle, possibly with a loop for the thumb. The small stone was then placed in the patch, the loose end of the string gripped in the hand and the whole sling whirled around the head until enough momentum had been worked up for the loose end to be released allowing the pebble to fly forward with very considerable force. On occasions special lead balls were cast for use by the slingers.

The javelin throwers carried only a very light shield which appears to have been wicker work with a layer

of animal skin, probably goat or sheep's hide. This small shield, or *pelta*, had an unusual, crescent shape and was carried with the two horns upwards. The javelins which were thrown were often fitted with a loop part of the way along the shaft to increase the power of the throw. The index and second finger were slipped into the loop whilst the shaft was held with the rest of the hand and this gave a little extra impetus in the forward direction when the javelin was thrown.

The Greeks did not make much use of the bow and its use seems to have been mainly confined to Cretan soldiers. The majority of arrowheads were flat with a large blade and a thick tang which stuck into the hole at the top of the shaft although a few are found with sockets to take the shaft. The most famous archers of this period were the Scyths who used a double recurved bow, the traditional cupid's bow. These archers used a very thin, light arrow and evidence from tombs suggests that they could carry as many as 200 or 300 arrows in the combined quiver and bow case which was known as the *gorytos*. The arrows were only about 18 inches long which suggests that the arrowheads were very small, probably not more than an inch or so in length. The shortness of the

arrow suggests that the power of these bows would have been fairly limited.

The Greeks used chariots in warfare from a very early date, although their use is thought to have been far more limited than some of the references in the *Iliad* suggest. A sixteenth century BC carving shows a warrior in a rather crude type of chariot drawn by one horse. A number of chariots were certainly kept at Knossos (*c.* 1500 BC) for tablets list over 400 attached to the palace. They were apparently stored in the armoury without their wheels for these are listed separately. A Cretan vase painting dating from the eleventh or tenth centuries gives us the first evidence for cavalry, which played an important part in warfare prior to the appearance of the hoplites around 700 BC. It is interesting to note that the hoplites – like many heavy troops in later ages – on occasion rode to battle, dismounted and formed their phalanx. Thessaly was famous for its cavalry and was frequently invited to supply units to its allies. There is evidence to suggest that some of the Greek cavalry horses were armoured for face-guards (or chamfrons as they are sometimes called) have been found in western Greece. Cavalry came to play a more important

part in later Greek history, particularly after the Peloponnesian wars (451–404 BC). Some time between 445 and 335 BC Xenophon gave the following description of the ideal cavalryman. He should have a light cuirass fitted with shoulder pieces, a neck-guard and gorget and an open-faced Boeotian helmet. Xenophon also recommends an arm-guard for the left hand which had to hold the reins; this would have been a kind of leather gauntlet extended from the shoulder to the fingers. For the right arm he suggests an ordinary light piece of armour. Xenophon took part in the march to Mesopotamia and gives some interesting details concerning both Greek and Persian archery. The archers of Crete had found themselves outranged by the Persians' longbow and Xenophon tells of a mountain people who used a longbow after the Turkish fashion, lying on their backs and using their feet to give greater power when drawing it. They seem to have fired an extremely heavy arrow which could pierce the Greek armour.

The Greek hoplite soldiers dominated the battlefields around the Mediterranean until the second century BC, during which time the Romans were becoming more powerful. At the Battle of Pydna

in 168 BC an army composed of the citizens of Rome turned the flank of a phalanx of spearmen from Macedonia, which was then the dominant power in the area. Rome gained the day by exploiting a basic weakness in this large body of men: its lack of manoeuvrability.

Rome, traditionally founded on the seven hills by the river Tiber in 753 BC, had grown from a small village into an expanding empire. The Roman army became the best organized military force in the ancient world and was made up of units known as legions. Their strength varied during the long span of Roman history but each usually had about 4500 to 5000 men, including a small number of cavalry. Each legion had one treasured possession in the form of a standard, or eagle. To lose the eagle in battle was the ultimate disgrace. The maximum number of legions maintained by Rome seems not to have exceeded 33; each was numbered and given a name and consisted of some 4000 men. Although all Roman citizens were liable to be called, many of the men who accepted the harsh life of the legion were volunteers and in 13 BC the length of service was set down to be twenty years. If they survived they received a grant of land on retirement.

One of the most important features of the Roman legion was the rigorous training demanded of soldiers and long hours were spent in learning to handle weapons. The legionary's spear, or *pilum*, was about 6 feet long and consisted of a wooden shaft with a long shank terminating in a small pyramidal head. Each legionary carried several *pila* and as he advanced into battle he hurled them at the enemy on the given command. The design was ingenious for the metal shank was of comparatively soft iron so that if the point failed to find a human target and struck the ground or buried itself in a shield, its own momentum and weight bent the iron shaft. This made it not only difficult to extract but also virtually impossible to hurl back at the advancing Roman legion. When the legionary had thrown his *pila* he drew his second weapon, the *gladius*. This was a short, broad-bladed, acutely pointed weapon intended purely for stabbing. The blade was about 20 inches long with a simple hilt and was carried in a sheath worn on the right hand side. To draw the sword, the legionary placed his hand round the hilt and then pulled down, so inverting the scabbard. This movement allowed a quick, easy draw, ready for instant action.

The Roman legionary of the first century BC was well protected for he had a sleeveless coat of mail which reached roughly to the middle of his thigh. The shoulders had extra strips crossing over them and the shirt was known as the *lorica hamata*.

Mail is very flexible and is made up of a number of small, connected rings. Each ring is interlocked with four others, two from the row above and two from the row below. It is a very old form of defence and seems to have originated in Gaul. The date when it was first used is uncertain but the earliest representation appears on a Roman monument dating from about the late third or early second century BC. Mail is difficult to make even when short cuts are used and to save time the Romans punched rings from metal and used these in alternate rows with handmade links

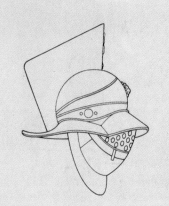

Opposite:
British shield of the late 1st century BC, of good quality and embossed with enamel.
British Museum, London.

Right:
The skull of a bronze, gold-covered helmet (4th century BC). The gold is further embellished with enamel decoration. A little extra protection is given by the small peak or neck guard. (Found at Amfreville.)
Musée du Louvre, Paris.

GLADIATORS

What began as a private form of dedication at a funeral became one of the world's most spectacular and sadistic events. For the Romans, gladiatorial games meant bloodshed. At first these combats were rare events. In 264 BC only three are recorded, but by 174 BC the number had risen to 74. The biggest change, however, came when two Roman Consuls sponsored a public display in 105 BC.

Most of the games were held in great arenas known as circuses which could be found dotted all over the Roman empire. Some, like the Colosseum in Rome, could hold up to 180,000 spectators. They had quarters for the combatants as well as cages for the large number of animals that were needed.

The men who fought in these games were known as gladiators; the name comes from the Latin word *gladius* meaning sword. Some were volunteers although most were slaves, prisoners of war and condemned criminals. Schools were established to ensure their fitness and teach them how to handle weapons. Before each series of games these fighters were feasted and indulged as they celebrated possibly their last day of life.

If they survived a tour of combats, usually three years, they were granted their freedom with a symbolic wooden sword.

At a typical series of games there was usually some parade and possibly some comic relief before the fights began. Some were straight contests between two men armed with sword and shield, others were more spectacular. The *retiarius* was armed with a three-pronged spear – the trident – and a fine meshed net but had no armour. The *murmillones* wore a jointed guard on the right arm, a greave on the left leg and a wide brimmed helmet with a tall comb. In some cases the men fought with their national weapons such as javelins, spears or even bows and arrows.

Later on, as the crowds tired of mere murderous matches between humans, variety, in the form of exotic animals, was introduced into the arena. Large numbers of creatures were captured and transported to Rome for the purpose of gladiatorial combat; in 249 AD the 1000th anniversary of the founding of Rome was celebrated by the slaughter of nearly 230 animals including lions and rhinoceroses, not to mention 2000 gladiators.

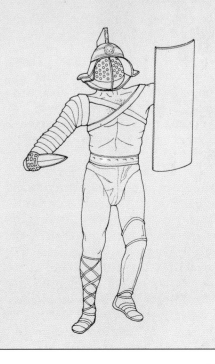

murmillones gladiatorial equipment

Remains of a *gladius* blade and scabbard.
The shortness of the blade meant that it
could be worn on the right-hand side
and still be drawn with the right hand.
British Museum, London.

joining the punched ones. These
connecting links were fashioned
from pieces of bronze and iron
wire the ends of which were flattened and pierced and then riveted
together after the ring was put in
place.

Not all the Roman legionaries
wore shirts of mail and the evidence
suggests that it was only the wealth-
ier who possessed one. The cavalry
are shown in mail and their *lorica
hamata* have slits at the side, obviously for greater ease and comfort on horseback. Although the
lorica hamata was later supplanted
by alternative forms of defence it
continued in use well on into the
third and fourth centuries AD, the

only difference being that the later
ones seem to have slightly larger
diameter links. From the centre
of a waist belt supporting dagger
and *gladius* there dangled a series
of leather straps with reinforcing
metal plates intended to protect the
vital organs.

The helmet of this period was of
bronze and is known as a jockey
cap. It had a dome shaped, bronze
skull with a flat peak which gave
some protection to the back of the
neck. The brow was further
strengthened by another, smaller
peak which sat an inch or so above
the brow and there were two large,
hinged ear flaps which were laced
and tied under the chin. It may be
that this style of helmet was developed in Gaul, probably by
armourers working in the Coolus
area of the Marne.

The legionary's defence was
completed by a large shield which
had originally been oval, but by this

period top and bottom had been
cut square so that it was now a
slightly curved, truncated oval
shape.

By the second half of the first
century AD the equipment had
begun to change and in place of the
old, bronze helmet the legionary
had an iron one which, although
basically the same, had been improved in some aspects. The rear
of the skull was now extended
further down to cover the back of
the head and neck and there was a
much wider sweep at the bottom to
give greater protection. There was
also a front peak. The cheek pieces
were slightly smaller with a space
cut out to leave the ear uncovered.
The helmet was far more elaborate
with applied decoration including
embossed, exaggerated eyebrows
set above the front peak. On top of
the skull an ornate crest holder
replaced the knob on the earlier,
bronze one.

The biggest change however was
in the body defence of the legionary who now wore a very ingenious,
efficient form of armour: the *lorica
segmentata*. This consisted of several
plates of metal riveted to inside
leather straps, and shaped to curve
over the body and shoulders. The
lorica segmentata was made in sections
which laced together to form the
complete armour. It was flexible,
allowing easy movement of the
arms and – very important for the
infantry – could quite easily be
packed away in a bag for carrying.
The construction was simple but
ingenious, consisting of some four-
teen curved plates for the trunk
and between eight and ten plates
for the shoulder. Where there was a
danger of a plate rubbing the skin
the edge was carefully curled over
to make it smooth. There were
differing patterns of the *lorica segmentata* which continued in use
for some considerable time. Generally the later models were
simplified versions of the earlier
style.

The Romans also used scale
armour, *lorica squamata*, and a variation of this, known as lamellar
armour, was made up of dozens of
narrow plates which, instead of
being secured to a base garment,
were simply laced together.

This relief from near the theatre at Epidaurus, Greece, shows a Roman cuirass which is shaped to suggest the muscles of the body. The Romans made great use of this form of bronze armour.

Another big change was in the shield which had now become the famous *scutum*, essentially rectangular in shape although curved round to protect the body. It was fitted with a large, rectangular boss with a central domed section. The legionary of this period still wore his *singulum* or military belt.

The helmet, although basically the same shape, had brass fittings and a simplified crest holder. It seems likely that all Roman helmets had some internal padding and this may have included a system of cords which could be adjusted to vary the size of lining so that the helmet would fit any head.

Several other types of helmet in addition to those already described were worn by the Roman troops.

The most striking of all was probably the so-called Cavalry Sports helmet which completely covered the head and had a very finely modelled face piece. It has been suggested that these were reserved for displays of horsemanship in freshly conquered territories or on the borders of the Empire, where it was desirable to impress the subjected races with the importance and strength of Rome. Other elaborate helmets and cuirasses moulded to suggest muscles were worn by officers with the same idea of impressing onlookers.

The western Roman Empire lasted for some four centuries but internal dissension and external pressures led to its final breakup. The old legion made up of native Roman citizens had largely been replaced by groups of mercenary auxiliary cavalry, formed from the Empire's subject races, and the whole of Western civilization was in danger of imminent collapse. Among the external pressures were attacks by sea raiders from the northern coast of Europe. In Britain the Romans had already taken steps to counter these sea-pirates and had set up a line of forts spaced out along the coast of eastern and southeastern England, in an attempt to beat off these Dark Age warriors. However, with the withdrawal of the Roman legions in the early part of the fifth century AD Britain was left, like her European neighbours, if not defenceless, less well organized to defend herself.

The Dark Ages

The latter period of the Roman Empire saw the migration of many peoples from their homeland. By the fifth century AD, much of Europe was occupied by various barbarian tribes – Goths, Visigoths, Huns, Vandals, Franks, Angles and Saxons – who had met with little resistance from the weakening Roman rule. Many of the new settlers had joined the Roman army as mercenary forces, and the internal dissensions of these various groups did much to weaken the West's most disciplined army.

One typical example of a group who became settlers is the Franks, who entered France in the fourth century as *foederati*, auxiliaries in the Roman forces. They came originally from Germany where they had acquired a reputation for frequent perjury. Tacitus, a Roman historian, writing late in the first century AD, says that only a few owned helmets or armour and most rode into battle naked or wearing only a cloak. Franks were essentially foot soldiers, but they made great use of throwing spears and later developed a throwing axe known as a *francisca*. The blade of the *francisca* was narrow at the neck where it fitted on to the haft and then swept gracefully down ending in a fairly narrow cutting edge. They also developed a spear called an *angon* which could be used as a thrusting weapon but which was primarily intended as a javelin. The head was barbed and the shaft was of soft iron so that, should it

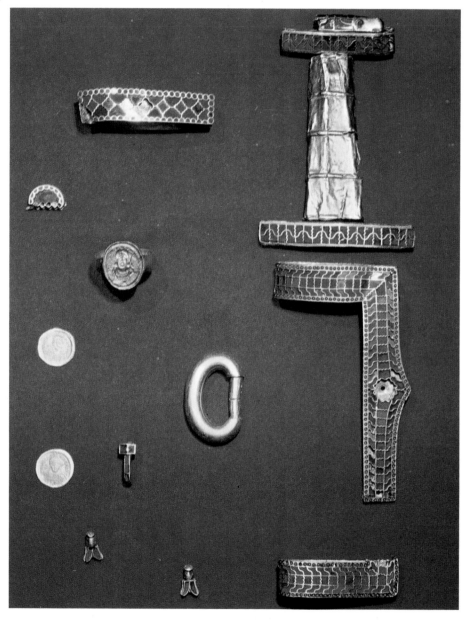

Sword fittings of gold and enamel found in a Merovingian tomb, *c.* 482, in France. *Cabinet des Medailles, Bibliothèque Nationale, Paris.*

miss its human mark and pierce a shield, it bent and was hard to pull out. (In this it can be compared with the Roman *pilum*.) A contemporary writer described how the Frank then rushed forward and placed his foot on the trailing shaft, thereby forcing his opponent to lower his shield and leave himself unprotected against a killing thrust.

Frankish chiefs must have possessed metal helmets, for remains have been found in graves near the Rhône. These helmets were fashioned from a series of T-shaped pieces, the short arms being linked to form a band while the longer arms were bent in to join at the top. The spaces were filled with plates of iron and a curtain of mail was fitted to guard the neck.

The Frankish swords of this period had a blade about 33 inches long which was double-edged and intended primarily for slashing. They were constructed by a method known as pattern-welding. Bars and rods of iron were heated and then cooled to harden the outside of the iron. These were then put between untreated rods which lacked the hardened surface and the entire metal sandwich was hammered together at one end. The sandwich was then twisted round to intertwine the hard and the soft bars, after which the whole thing was hammered and welded into one. Hardened rods were then hammered into place round the outside edges of the twisted, beaten bar to ensure that the cutting edge would be hard. Finally the entire blade was heated and plunged into water or oil before being reheated and allowed to cool naturally. The blade was now shaped, polished and sharpened. Pattern-welding was used from the second century until the tenth and it has been suggested that it was developed because it was not easy to produce single pieces of iron large enough to work into a blade. Whatever the

The head of a *francisca* or throwing axe, a popular weapon with the Franks. This example probably dates from the 6th–7th centuries AD.

Tradition has it that this sword once belonged to Charlemagne (768–814 AD) but it is almost certainly later – probably 12th century although possibly earlier. It was used at the coronation of the kings of France.
Musée du Louvre, Paris.

This stele was carved by a Frankish sculptor in Westphalia at Neiderdollendorf during the 7th or 8th century AD. The warrior carries what could well be a scramasax.

reason for its use the result was a blade which was sharp and hard but not so brittle that it would break on impact.

During the fifth century a large, single-edged knife known as a *scramasax* appears which was carried in a scabbard of leather folded over with the edges riveted together. The *scramasax* or *seax*, which was also common to the Saxons and Vikings, is a term used to cover a whole range of single-edged weapons. Although there are variations in the shape of the blade, they consist basically of a broad back which rises slightly from the line parallel to the cutting edge and then slopes acutely down to the point of the sword.

By the late ninth and early tenth centuries sword blades had changed in shape and had a slight taper from hilt to point. This changed the balance of the weapon and made it easier to handle as well as permitting greater use of the point for stabbing. Swords were now about 38 inches long.

At around the same time as the Franks occupied France, Britain herself was undergoing the first of a series of invasions. Tradition has it that the first of the Saxons arrived at the invitation of a local king who had the idea that they would protect the country from further attack by other Saxons. The reverse proved to be the case for the Saxons invited in their friends and began to take over. Despite opposition the Saxons acquired more and more of the country, and most of Britain finally succumbed. Only in Wales and Cornwall did the native Celtic culture manage to hold its own.

The Saxons were great fighters and their chief weapon in the early days, judging by the numbers found in graves of the period, was the spear. This was around 6 feet long and had a shaft of ash, a socketed iron spearhead and a metal tip, the ferrule, at the end of the shaft. Most of the spearheads are plain although a few have some applied metal decoration. The design of the spear was such that it could be used either as a thrusting weapon or as a javelin and there are indications that at a later date the Saxon warrior was normally armed with two or three spears some of which were javelins.

Swords are far less frequently found in the graves but this does not necessarily mean that they were less often used but rather that they were considered too

Left:
The remains of a helmet excavated from an Anglo Saxon burial mound in Derbyshire. On the top is the same boar figure as is seen on Viking helmets. Such helmets are described in the Anglo-Saxon poem Beowulf.
Sheffield City Museum.

Below:
The leader of this group of Carolingian soldiers carries a dragoon banner whilst the others are armed with long-headed spears. They carry round shields and wear mail hauberks and simple 'kettle' hats. From a Swiss psalter, 841–872 AD.
Stifts-Bibliothek, St. Gallen.

Left:
Helmet from a pre-Viking grave in Vendel, Sweden. It consists of a metal skull with a mail face-guard, and has applied decoration. Probably 6th–7th century.
Upplandsmuseet, Uppsala.

41

valuable to be left in the grave with the dead warrior. That the Saxons valued their swords is beyond doubt for in the middle of the tenth century one sword was considered the equivalent of 120 oxen or fifteen slaves. The early Saxon blade had edges roughly parallel which then curved into a not very acute point. There was a groove down the centre of the flat part of the blade to reduce the weight without sacrificing rigidity. Some of the swords of this period have a ring attached to the pommel and its function is not clear; some argue that it was a mark of royal favour, others that it had some connection with taking an oath on the sword. Another weapon commonly found in Saxon graves is the seax or scramasax; some of these are long enough to justify being called a short sword.

The Saxon shield was of wood; it often had a covering of animal skin and occasionally it was strengthened with an iron bar or with iron strips around the edge. It was held by means of a central bar, the hole to accommodate the knuckles being covered by a dome. The Saxons seem to have possessed little armour although there is some evidence of the use of mail.

The Saxon dominance over Britain reached its peak with Alfred the Great, who was born *c.* 848 and crowned king of Wessex in 871. During his reign he fought many battles against a new set of invaders, this time coming from Scandinavia: fierce and daring seamen known as the Vikings. The name 'Viking' means a pirate wandering in search of plunder, and it is this aspect which has captured popular imagination, although in addition to

Excavated in 1904 at Oseberg, this is a well preserved example of a 9th-century Viking ship. It is 76½ feet (approx. 23 metres) long and 17½ feet (approx. 5 metres) wide at the beam, and has no fixed deck. The ship was steered by a large oar mounted on the starboard side at the stern.
Norsk Folke Museum, Bygdøy, Oslo.

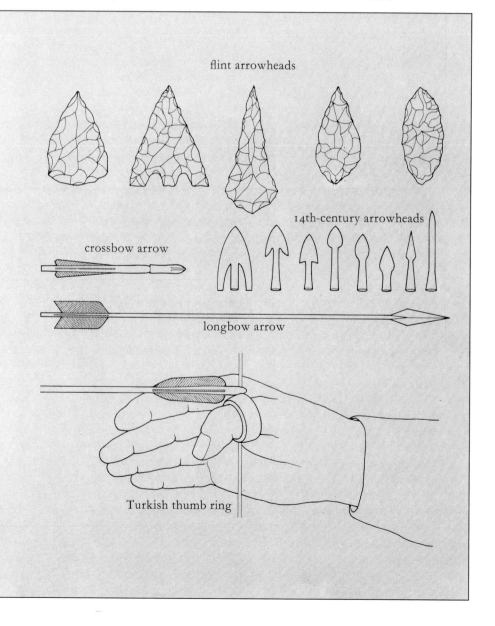

ARROWS and ARCHERY
Flint was used by Stone Age men and many societies for their arrowheads, but it was later replaced by metal. The Ancient Greeks used small, socketed, bronze heads and, later on, iron and steel were used. Until the thirteenth century the same type of arrow seems to have been used both for war and hunting but as armour became tougher special shapes were designed to give a better penetration. From the fourteenth century onwards nearly all war arrows had rather thin heads with very little swell towards the socket. This shape ensures that the maximum punch is delivered on the smallest area so that the penetrating force is at its greatest. For hunting most of the arrows were barbed so that the head was unlikely to fall out. The arrow for the longbow was about a yard long and fletched with goose feathers. Crossbow bolts were shorter and thicker and had wood or leather vanes.

Most archers wore a guard known as a bracer on their left arm to protect them against the slap of the bow string. On their right hand European archers often had some form of finger guard. Asiatic bowmen used a different kind of hold for the bowstring and wore an archers' ring on their thumb. The string was held by the ring and not by the three fingers as in Europe.

flint arrowheads

crossbow arrow

14th-century arrowheads

longbow arrow

Turkish thumb ring

A scramasax blade, probably of Saxon origin, 9th or 10th century. 10½ inches (26.7 cm).

raiding and settling in countries as far apart as Ireland, Iceland, Spain, France and Russia, they had a fine indigenous culture. The first recorded assault on Britain occurred in the year 769. Somewhere off the Dorset coast, in the south of England, three ships appeared. If excavated examples are any guide they were probably more than 75 feet long with a graceful prow that curved upwards to culminate in a fearsome carving. About 17 feet wide at the centre and remarkably shallow, they had a mast 40 feet high from which hung a red and white sail of wool. There was provision for 16 oars a side and each ship held approximately sixty men. When the three long ships were sighted a royal servant, the King's Reeve, rode down to the beach to enquire as to the business of the crews. The only answer he received was, presumably, the short, sharp cut of a sword, for it is recorded that he was killed.

This incident was the first of many raids by the Vikings, who excelled in the surprise attack. When they landed they usually fought on foot, but they would round up every available horse in order to increase the speed with which they surprised the enemy.

The earliest of the raiders seem to have relied, as did their Saxon opponents, chiefly on the sword and spear, although they were later to acquire a deserved reputation for their use of the terrible Danish axe. The axe was at first

the everyday tool of the ordinary farmer but as the potential of these weapons was realized, special shapes were developed. The 'bearded axe' had a squarish projection at the top of the axehead which meant that it could be used both in battle and on the land. The broad axe was designed solely as a weapon and had a blade with a wide cutting edge. The blade was mounted on a shaft of between 6 and 7 feet long, which was reinforced with iron strips to reduce the chances of its being chopped or hacked by an enemy blade. It was a fairly heavy weapon which meant that it was almost certainly held in both hands. The cutting power of the head at the end of a sweeping, two-handed stroke must have been great enough to slash through any shield or armour of the period. It was a weapon greatly to be feared and one revered by the Vikings themselves.

The Viking sword, like the earlier Bronze Age weapon, was essentially for cutting rather than thrusting. The hilt was simple with a comparatively small, straight cross-guard, known as the quillon. The grip was usually of wood, perhaps covered with leather or bound with wire. A small, solid metal block, known as the pommel, was fitted on the top of the grip and served as a counter-balance to the blade; this came in a variety of shapes. The sword hilts were usually plain but some decorated ones have been found. The blade was like that of the Frankish sword, constructed by the pattern-welding method. The hammering and twisting of pattern welding produced a striking surface pattern. Contemporary accounts make frequent references to this effect which rather resembled the mottled skin of a snake. Many of the sagas and legends of the Vikings compare the quick move-

Top left:
Carvings on this memorial stone at Klintebys, Gotland, depict a Viking long ship with a square sail and a warrior on horseback.

Bottom left:
Carvings on this stone from Gotland, Sweden show warriors with swords and round shields.

Top right:
Head of a Viking battle-axe found in the Thames at London. This shape, with its wide, slightly angled, cutting edge would, when mounted on a long shaft, ensure a really terrible cut.
The Museum of London.

Bottom right:
Head of Danish axe with its great cutting edge. This is the type shown on the Bayeux Tapestry.
British Museum, London.

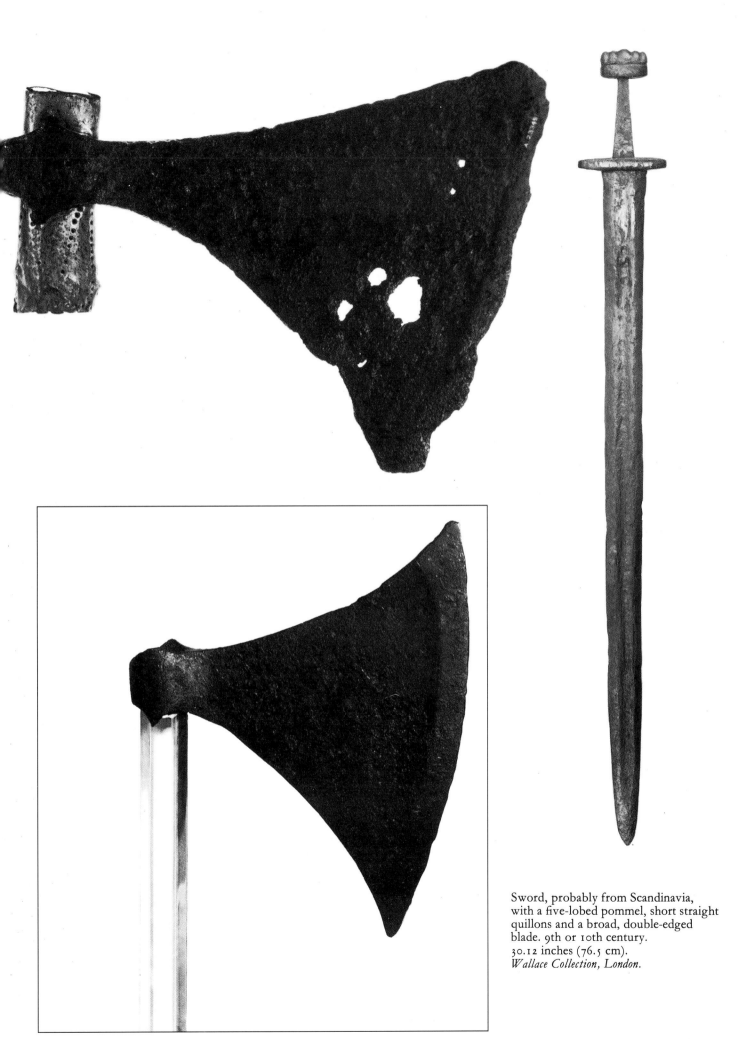

Sword, probably from Scandinavia,
with a five-lobed pommel, short straight
quillons and a broad, double-edged
blade. 9th or 10th century.
30.12 inches (76.5 cm).
Wallace Collection, London.

ment of the sword with the sting of a snake.

If the combination of hard and soft metals, the welding, the hammering, the heating and the softening were just right then a sword blade of superb quality was produced. Such a blade became a treasured possession to be passed on to an heir. Some bladesmiths acquired a reputation for their work and maker's names such as Inglerii and Ulfberht are found worked into the metal as a guarantee of quality. Blade and grip were united by means of the tang – a long, narrow projection at the end of the blade. The tang passed through the components of the hilt and the tip was then hammered over the pommel making a firm and lasting join. The sword was carried in a scabbard, but because of its length the Viking sword could not be drawn in the same way as the Roman *gladius*. It was therefore carried on the left-hand side and drawn across the body with the right hand. Evidence suggests that the early Vikings carried their scabbards on a baldric which was worn over the right shoulder, but later it seems that a waist belt became much more common. The scabbard was sometimes decorated by applied

46

Carved wooden posts from Hyllestad,
Sweden, with scenes from the story of
Sigurd the Dragon Slayer, one of the
Viking sagas. The two figures on the
bottom right are shown making Sigurd's
sword.

metalwork. The blade was particularly susceptible to rust when exposed to the salt sea air and it was
common practice, as with the
Romans, to line the scabbard with
materials which would inhibit the
rust.

Some warriors carried a spear in
addition to their sword or axe.
This usually had a rather long spearhead attached to the shaft by means
of a socket. Spearheads are commonly found on Viking sites in
Scandinavia and the variety of
sizes and shapes suggests that some
were designed specifically for
throwing whilst others were for
stabbing. Some of the throwing
spears seem to have been fitted
with some form of grip near the
middle of the shaft to facilitate a
firm hold. There are also references
to twisting spears which suggest
that the spears were in some way
spun so as to increase their accuracy. Like all warriors the Vikings
delighted in their martial skills and
the sagas make great play of the
hero who was able to cast spears
equally well with the right or the
left hand. Another feat was to
catch a spear in flight and, using
its momentum, turn it to continue
its flight back to its original owner.
It seems likely that the throwing
spear was the more common for
there are frequent references to
them in the sagas.

When armour was worn it was
almost invariably mail rather than
scale. The mail coat was known as
the *byrnie* or *hringskyrta*, but it is
unlikely that all Vikings had mail
and the evidence suggests that most
wore some form of padded leather
coat. Leather is very resistant to
cuts and a double layer with some
moss, hay or wool packed between
would make an efficient and comparatively cheap form of defence.
There are references in the sagas to
this form of padded armour.

According to tradition, the helmet of the Vikings is bedecked with
horns and wings. A form of horned
head-dress does appear in some
Viking carvings but whether these
are fighting helmets or, as would
seem more likely from their con-
text, some form of religious
decoration, is not clear. What can
be said with certainty is that the

vast majority of Viking helmets are much less elaborate than this. The usual helmet was conical and without horns or other appendages. Some were fitted with a simple nasal bar whereas others, presumably belonging to leaders and more prosperous members of the community, had far more elaborate facial protection. Some, particularly those from Sweden, had a domino-like face-piece and two large ear flaps. This elaborate style of helmet seems to have been used only in the very early period of the Viking age.

Another piece of defensive equipment of the Viking warrior was a round shield, which was hung on a rail running round the side of the ship until it was required for battle. The shield was made of a series of short planks, secured by some form of crossbar, and was held in one hand by means of this bar. Although sometimes painted and decorated, they were of a fairly rough construction since they were considered expendable. Some were, no doubt, strengthened with layers of hide; others with metal. The shield was not solely defensive and could be used almost as a weapon. The skill in using a shield was to catch an opponent's blade in such a way that it would be deflected without damaging the shield. Skilful use of the sword and shield was designed to force an opponent into a position where he was unable to use his shield. This was undoubtedly to the detriment of the latter and in a formal duel the rules permitted a total of three shields to be used in any one combat.

This fine Viking sword was part of a burial in which several swords had been bent in the same way as part of the burial ritual.
Statens Historiska Museum, Stockholm.

Some warriors known as the Berserks or the Wolfskins who were perhaps members of a religious sect devoted to the Viking god Odin, disdained all forms of defence. Accounts speak of them working themselves into a passion by dancing and chanting, and, once they had generated a sense of elation, charging against the enemy ignoring weapons and wounds until they were either victorious or dead.

Descendants of the Vikings settled in France around the mouth of the Seine and in Normandy, the land of the Northmen. A descendant of these warriors, William the Bastard, was to become yet another invader: William the Conqueror, who became king of England after the Battle of Hastings in 1066.

The Battle of Hastings was fought over a dispute over the

English throne. William claimed that he had been promised it by Edward the Confessor. The English ruling body (the *Witan* or *Witangemot*) however decreed that it should go to Harold, son of Godwin. William therefore decided to attack, and, towards the end of September, 1066, a change of wind enabled him to launch his armada against the south coast of England, and he landed his troops near the town now called Pevensey. Harold, who had already that month had to fight a Viking invasion in the north of England, was forced to march south again before he had time to rest and re-group. The famous battle was fought on the hill of Senlac on October 14th 1066. Accounts of the battle differ but victory came to the Normans when they succeeded in breaking the Saxon line. Whether the break was caused by a trick of William's or whether Harold's men disobeyed orders and broke ranks, will never be known. Sufficient to say that at the end of the day William was victorious and Harold was dead.

These dies were used to stamp out metal plates for helmets. The warrior on the top left is armed with sword and dagger whilst those on the top right have spears. The man on the bottom left wears a horned helmet whilst the one on the bottom right carries an axe. The dies were found at Oland, Sweden and are pre-Viking.
Statens Historiska Museum, Stockholm.

This detail from a 12th-century Viking tapestry shows a warrior very similar to those featured on the Bayeux tapestry. The helmet has the long nasal, the shield is kite-shaped, and the rider wears a hauberk.
Kunstindustrimuseet, Oslo.

The Early Middle Ages

The historian is fortunate in that there is a near-contemporary pictorial record of the events before, during and after the Battle of Hastings. The Bayeux Tapestry, which is not a tapestry but an embroidery, tells the story from the Norman side. The figures are detailed and their accuracy is, in general, confirmed by other sources.

The Norman host was essentially a cavalry army, and Hastings was a classic example of a battle between mounted troops and infantry. The cavalry won because, as on many other occasions, the infantry failed to hold their lines – a fatal mistake. Harold's defence depended upon his army being able to hold its formation against the onslaught of Norman cavalry charges.

The Norman warrior of 1066 was well equipped and for the next few decades changes were few. The main body defence remained the coat of mail known as the hauberk which was worn over a long, sturdy tunic. This must have been very necessary for otherwise the links of the mail would have rubbed and pinched the skin, caught hairs and generally been thoroughly uncomfortable. The hauberk reached only to the knee and to permit a horseman to mount and ride the front and back were split roughly down to the crotch. If the Bayeux Tapestry is to be believed then most hauberks had only elbow length sleeves although one or two are shown with full length sleeves.

Some hauberks were modified so that the sword was worn under the mail with just the hilt projecting. One puzzling feature of virtually every hauberk shown on the Bayeux Tapestry is a clearly delineated square shape on the chest. Whether this represents some form of reinforcing or whether it is an opening is not clear and so far no acceptable explanation has been offered.

The legs were largely unprotected although they appear covered

A detail from the Bayeux Tapestry showing a Saxon soldier (left) wielding a long handled Danish axe, while the horsemen hold their shields and ply their swords with vigour.

This plaque from Le Mans cathedral shows Count Geoffrey of Anjou, who was the father of Henry II, king of England (1154–1189). His shield is of the typical Norman kite shape and is painted with a series of heraldic lions or leopards, one of which is also on his cap.

The Four Horsemen of the Apocalypse are shown in this manuscript from Spain, dating from the turn of the 11th century. All four wear hauberks. *British Museum, London.*

with mail in some contemporary illustrations. Later leggings of mail, known as hosen, were worn over some kind of stocking or padded leg covering and were, no doubt, supported by a strap or thong tied to a waist belt. There was another less elaborate form of leg defence which consisted of a strip of mail placed over the front of the leg and laced up behind.

The hauberk was extended to incorporate a hood, known as the coif, which covered the head but left the face bare. There must have been some cap or cloth hood or a lining fixed inside the coif to prevent the discomfort of links rubbing against the unprotected head. Over the coif went the helmet which was often the same as that worn by the Franks. It had a series of bars uniting to form a conical frame, the spaces of which were filled in with sheets of horn or metal. A distinctive feature of the

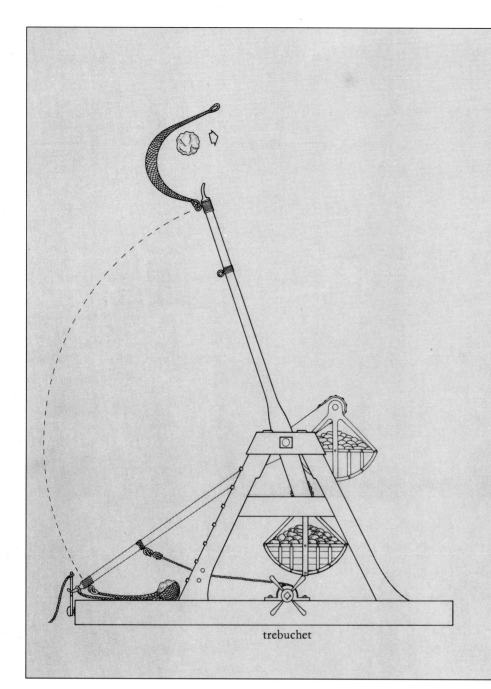

trebuchet

TREBUCHET

As castle walls were made higher and stronger in the Middle Ages, the old methods of attack were no longer sufficient. Scaling ladders and siege towers were used but these were hazardous. An assault was more likely to succeed if an actual breech could be made in the wall. Battering rams were effective but they were difficult to get into position against the walls and even if a cover was built over the ram it was still rather exposed. Mining was a very reliable method but as it often involved the digging of very long tunnels, it could be a slow business. A better solution was to knock a hole in the wall by some kind of missile.

The mangonel, one form of catapult, had a long, wooden arm which was kept under tension by a twisted skein of sinew or rope. The arm was pulled down by a windlass and a large stone placed at the end of the arm. The arm was then released and sprang forward to hit the frame and so send the stone flying through the air. In the twelfth century a more complicated form of catapult, the trebuchet, became common. A long arm with a sling at one end was counter-balanced by a heavy weight at the other. The arm was winched down and a stone, weighing between two and three hundredweight, placed in the sling. The arm was then released and the counterweight pulled the arm down, sending the missile on a high trajectory over or into the wall.

helmet was the nasal which was a broad bar projecting down over the face, reaching probably to just below the tip of the nose. Whilst this was little protection against a stab it certainly offered some against a cut from a sword. Another version of this helmet was made in one piece with the nasal, or face bar, riveted on separately. The feet were unprotected apart from leather shoes and the horseman wore a pair of simple spurs which were little more than a spike fitted to the back of a U-shaped piece of metal, laced or strapped on to the foot.

The weapons which had served the Normans well at Hastings remained largely unchanged for many years. Their sword was virtually the same as that of the Vikings with a double-edged blade which tapered to a point and a simple, straight crossguard. The grip was covered with leather or wire and the pommel was rather like an inverted D. The archers who had played an important role in the battle carried their fairly short arrows in a quiver which either hung from a baldric over the shoulder or was attached to a waist belt. The bow was fairly short and seems to have been drawn only to the chest which suggests that its power was limited. In addition to the ordinary longbow the Normans and other European archers made use of the crossbow, which had one great advantage in that it could be spanned (made ready to discharge an arrow) and left in that condition until required. A long, wooden bar known as the stock had at one end the bowstaff which was set at right angles to it. The thick cord was attached to the staff and could be pulled back until it engaged with a small, shaped, pivotted block known as the nut, set in the shaft. When the string engaged with the nut it locked in place so that the bow was held under tension. A crossbow arrow, short and rather thick, was placed in a groove in front of the cord. When ready the crossbowman depressed a lever beneath the stock which allowed the nut to rotate,

disengaging the string which then drove the arrow forward. The spear or lance was still very popular and was used either in the overarm position for stabbing or else tucked under the arm for a charge.

Although his mail gave a fair degree of protection, the left-hand side of a horseman was vulnerable. His right hand being occupied with his weapons, he had to hold his reins in the left, which meant that he could do little to protect that side of his body. The shield that the Normans developed was kite-shaped and long enough to cover a rider from shoulder to foot. It was fitted at the back with a long strap to allow it to be hung over

the neck or at the side. There were several shorter straps through which the left arm could be slipped. The shield itself was of wood although there was apparently greater use of metal reinforcing.

During the next century or so the basic body defences were little changed. The hauberk was made slightly longer, reaching to the knee or a little below. The coif was made looser fitting and probably had some padding in the top part. When not required – it must have been rather uncomfortable and stuffy to wear – it could be thrown back from the head to hang down over the shoulders. Attached to the right-hand side of the coif, where it joined the neck, was a

flap of mail which was drawn across the chin and side of the face and then tied in position with a leather thong. Arm defences were developed and the hauberk sleeves now reached to the wrist and often included a pair of mittens. The mittens had mail only on the back of the hand whilst the palm was covered by a piece of hard wearing cloth or leather. The palm was slit so that the mittens could be slipped off for comfort. Leg mail was more common during the twelfth century now covering the whole of the foot and reaching up beyond the lower edge of the hauberk.

A padded garment, known as a *gambeson* or *aketon*, was worn beneath the mail hauberk and this was sometimes used on its own as a form of armour, rather like that of the early Vikings. Scale armour which had been so very popular seems to have gone out of fashion

although it was occasionally used and examples are shown in a few contemporary illustrations.

From the middle of the twelfth century a sleeveless, waisted linen gown is shown on many monuments and in illustrations. At first it was quite plain but from the thirteenth century the device shown on shields is repeated on the gowns. The purpose of this gown is not clear for the protection it gave to mail and man was minimal. It is possible that it was just a fashion copied from the Saracens as a result of the Crusades.

The helmet shown on the Bayeux tapestry continued to be worn for some considerable time but by the end of the century other types are shown on various monuments. Some were round-topped and a few were cylindrical and flat-topped. This latter development is rather surprising since a flat top defeats one of the main purposes of

Above:
German sword of the late 12th century. The pommel is of the typical 'brazil nut' shape of the period. The blade is double-edged and has a wide fuller (groove) along each side.
Wallace Collection, London.

Opposite top:
The Emperor Charlemagne (800–814 AD) is depicted mourning dead knights on this carved box panel from Aachen cathedral. The flat topped helmets, mail leggings and shields would suggest a date of late 12th or early 13th century for the carving.

Opposite bottom:
This illustration from the famous Maciejowski Bible shows a scene of war and is interesting for the diversity of arms and armour it portrays. The knights wear mail and a variety of helmets while the defenders of the castle wear kettle hats. (Mid-13th century.)
MS 638 folio 10v. The Pierport Morgan Library, New York.

Right:
Young Offa's spear passes through shield and mail in this spirited illustration to 'The Lives of Two Offas' by Matthew Paris c. 1250.
British Museum, London.

armour, which should not only give direct protection but which should also deflect as well as stop the cut of an assailant's weapon. The nasal which was the only face-guard on the Norman helmet was developed, and by the first quarter of the twelfth century helmets are shown with extensions covering the back of the head, whereas around the end of the twelfth century more elaborate face-guards are illustrated. These are rather mask-like and extend from the brim down to the mouth. Another style of helmet first illustrated during this century is the kettle hat: the name is derived from the

cauldron, a large bowl with an outward curving brim, which was then known as a kettle. This style of helmet was simple to construct as well as cheap and efficient and remained in use for centuries.

As other body defences were improved the need for a shield decreased and the long, kite shield of the Normans was reduced in size. Lances were used less often in the overarm position but were now usually tucked under the arm: this is known as couching. It became common practice to hang the shield round the neck from the long strap whilst using the lance; the arm straps were only used when

the lance had been discarded in battle and the sword was in action. Couching was effective but it was difficult to maintain a firm grip on the lance if the target was hit. Early in the twelfth century, armourers began fitting a large disc near the end of the staff which would be in direct contact with the shoulder when the lance was couched; the effect of this disc was to enable the rider to absorb the shock of impact.

The sword changed little during the thirteenth century although the blade became slightly longer. The crossguard was normally straight although some had a slight

curve towards the point. Towards the end of the century the pommel changed, becoming round instead of D-shaped or brazil nut-shaped.

The terrible, long handled Danish axe seems to have fallen from favour, but a shorter version with a haft some three to four feet long is frequently depicted on the monuments or in illustrations.

Mail was a simple, effective means of defence but it was not without limitations. The hauberk was uncomfortable to wear since its entire weight was carried on the shoulders. Mail may have stopped a cut but it would still transmit the force of a blow sufficient to break a bone or

produce a very nasty bruise. The rings were far less effective against a thrust and a penetrating cut could drive broken links into a wound. In the unhygienic conditions of the period infection would almost certainly have been the result.

Armourers were no doubt under pressure from the knights to improve their defences and it is during the thirteenth century that the beginnings of plate armour, made up of larger pieces of metal, are seen. Mail was not to be discarded for many centuries but it was gradually supplanted and fell from being a principal to a secondary defence. Coifs were now either

part of the hauberk or made separately and were usually worn over a padded cap. From the middle of the thirteenth century there is evidence to suggest that the coif was lined and one contemporary writer mentions the use of fur for such a lining. Extra protection at the neck and throat was achieved by a reinforcing scarf of mail, possibly strengthened with small metal plates. The skill of the mail maker was now considerable and there are references to mail gloves with fingers. In parts of Europe small metal plates were being used to make the gauntlets which protected the hands.

59

HERALDIC DEVICES

When the helmet left the face uncovered it was not difficult to recognize friend or foe, but as armour covered more and more of the face and body, this became a serious problem. The middle of a battle was no time or place to stop and check identities. To overcome this serious difficulty a system of signs and badges developed. From earliest times shields had been painted with patterns and pictures but there had been no system and the choice had been haphazard. The concept of the regular use of some identifying mark developed slowly but by the late twelfth century it seems to have become a fairly well established practice.

In Britain one of the first moves towards a royal coat of arms is seen on a seal of Richard I (1188–1199) which was probably made in 1194. It shows the king with his shield decorated with the royal lions – in fact they are leopards – which are also repeated on a fan-like crest fitted to the top of his helmet. By the early thirteenth century it was quite common for such badges or patterns to be painted on the side of the helmet.

Some knights are shown in illustrations with their chosen emblem modelled in relief and mounted on top of the helmet.

From this simple beginning a very complex and involved system of family and town badges and patterns evolved with very rigid rules. A central feature of these 'arms' was the shield; the most common shape was that known as the 'flat iron' with a straight top to the shield. There were many other shaped shields all with their own names. Each shield was divided into sections each with its own special name which must always be used when describing or 'blazoning' the arms. It was usually coloured, and the nine basic colours, known as tinctures, are two metals, gold and silver, five colours, red, blue, black, green and purple and two furs, ermine and vair (squirrel). Each of these tinctures has its own heraldic name as does the object drawn on the field or part of the shield.

The shield might be divided into sections by a whole range of stripes and curves, and again each form has its own special name. As more and more families adopted these coats of arms, so it became necessary to devise more and more distinctions and the whole subject of heraldry became extremely involved with a language all of its own (there are, for example, fifteen different crosses used in heraldry). The whole system became so complex that disputes were frequent and special courts were set up to deal with these very involved cases. Special permission was necessary before any change was made to the arms and new coats of arms were only granted after careful checks to ensure that they did not copy any existing arms.

The legs of the cavalryman are particularly vulnerable for they are within easy reach of a foot soldier. During the second quarter of the thirteenth century many of the horsemen fitted padded guards over their thighs and from about 1220–30 the monuments and manuscripts begin to show small metal plates fitted at the knee and secured to the quilted thigh pieces.

It seems fairly certain that early in the thirteenth century some form of body armour was being worn on the Continent but its use does not appear to have reached England until the second half of the century. The earliest form was almost certainly a garment fitted with fairly large plates, rather in the style of scale armour, and worn over the hauberk. Discs of metal were also fitted at the elbow and at the shoulder to give greater protection at these vulnerable points. The shield was reduced in size over the century and was now comparatively small.

Great changes had taken place in the design of the helmet and the conical type with extra pieces fitted to guard the neck and face had developed until, by the middle of the century, the helmet completely enclosed the head. It was almost certainly padded on the inside where there were laces or straps to hold it firmly in position on the head. It was roughly cylindrical in shape and had two narrow slits for vision and a number of holes in the lower part to allow air to circulate inside. It was fashioned from several pieces and the joins were often reinforced.

Top:
A detail from a sculptured group depicting the Massacre of the Innocents, dating from the second half of the 13th century and situated in the north cloister of Notre Dame, Paris. The soldiers wear mail coifs and mittens. The swords have the D-shaped pommel common at this period and a blade with a single, central fuller.
Notre Dame, Paris.

Above:
13th-century sword with slightly down-curving quillons and tapering blade. 33.37 inches (84.8 cm).
Wallace Collection, London.

Not all the troops were able to afford the very expensive defences listed above and infantry and poorer knights would often have been equipped with a gambeson and perhaps a simple domed helmet or kettle hat.

As the strong defences were developed so the armourers sought to develop stronger or more efficient weapons. During the thirteenth century larger swords became more common with a grip big enough to be held in both hands, permitting a much harder swing. Quillons were commonly straight although some had a slight down curve towards the point. The pommel was usually circular although spheres and other more complex shaped blocks were used. In an effort to develop greater cutting power single-edged blades became fashionable. The falchion was one of the more popular forms and was designed to have the maximum weight at a point where it would have the greatest effect: consequently the blade was much wider near the point, so as to give a good cut.

Although this sword is very ornate with gold enamelling and semi-precious stones, the shape is characteristic of the 13th century. It was used when Frederick II of Austria was crowned as Holy Roman Emperor in 1220. *Kunsthistorisches Museum, Vienna.*

Apart from weapons that gave a much more powerful cut, another answer to the improved defences was a stabbing weapon to attack vulnerable points, and it is during this century that special thrusting swords were developed. Their blades had virtually no cutting edge and the point was often thickened so that the weapon was almost a miniature spear. These *estocs* were designed for use in close combat when they could be driven home at a poorly protected spot on the warrior. Daggers, very similar in design to the larger swords, were now part of the knight's armoury and were normally carried on the left hand side of the belt. Clubs, or maces, and axes were still commonly used and the long handled axe seems to have returned to favour.

The fourteenth century was of outstanding importance for both armourers and weapon makers for it was during this period that the longbow, which had long been in use, became a dominant factor on the battlefield. The longbow was basically very simple, even rather crude, in design. The staff was about 6 feet in length. It was thick at the centre and thinned slightly towards the ends where there would have been either a cut into the wood or a horned tip with a slot cut in it. Into these nocks went the looped end of a flax bowstring. The fixing of the string into position required some considerable degree of strength and skill and it was only done prior to action, the bow normally being carried unstrung.

The arrows were about 36 inches long; the feathers were important and the best results were thought to come from goose feathers. The war arrow was very acutely pointed and therefore achieved great penetration by delivering maximum impact on a minimum area. In battle the archer could release a steady flow of arrows into the air and the effect of several hundred archers maintaining this continuous stream must have been devastating. To keep up the speed of the attack the arrows were either pushed into the belt or stuck point down in the ground in front of the archer. Skilful use of the longbow depended upon the correct co-ordination of the body as the bow was drawn. The arrow was nocked (which means that the string was fitted into a slot at the end of the arrow), the string was drawn back as the bow was raised, the bow aimed, and the arrows released almost in one continuous, smooth movement. Since the bow required a pull of some 80 pounds, it would have been very difficult, if not impossible, for the average archer to have held the bow in a steady, aiming position: thus quick release was unavoidable. There are numerous contemporary stories of the terrible effects of these arrows; oak doors 4 inches thick were pierced almost as easily as paper and men were transfixed. Armourers sought means to counter this new weapon and the fourteenth century saw the development of much more plate armour.

The first apparent difference in armour of this period is the use of semi-tubular plates, which are strapped onto the lower and upper sections of the arm. These had a double effect: firstly, the force of a blow was now dispersed over a much wider area and the danger of broken bones and bruising was thus reduced; secondly the smoother surface had more chance of deflecting a blow rather than merely absorbing it. This 'glance' technique became very important and the old, rather barrel-shaped helmet was soon replaced with one with a gracefully tapering skull, again primarily designed to deflect the edge of a sword. A great

Rubbing of a monumental brass of Sir William Fitzralph at the church of Pebmarch, Essex. It dates from the early 14th century and clearly indicates the gradual introduction of plate. Arms and legs now have additional protection in the form of plates as do the top of the feet, and round plates add to the defences at elbow and shoulder: but mail is still very important. The sword belt has a very elaborate fastening.

Sir John de Creke, c. 1325, has more plate defence with a metal helmet and what appears to be some form of extra defences on the chest.

Sir Peter Courtenay, 1409, has a full harness of plate with a mail fitting to the bascinet. His gauntlets are fashioned from plates and his belt carries a dagger and a sword. His great helm with a crest rests behind his head.

An early 14th-century joust with musicians playing in the balcony. The ring and vamplate on the lances are clearly shown and the tip of the broken lance has a coronel. The small shields and horse trappings carry heraldic devices.
Manesse Codex Universitätsbibliothek, Heidelberg.

variety of helmets were in use at this time although some knights preferred still to wear just a coif of mail under a kettle hat. Some retained their barrel-shaped helms whilst others preferred the newer type which had a pivotted face-piece, the visor. One of the discomforts of wearing a helmet was the lack of fresh air and the ability to raise a visor for some cooling air must have been very welcome. These great, visored helmets with the sloping top were known as bascinets, a term used for many differing styles of helmet. The earliest form of bascinet was usually just the simple metal cap, often worn under a conventional helm. The bascinets often had a curtain of mail fitted around the lower edge so that the throat and shoulders were protected. This curtain of mail was

sometimes replaced by a piece of plate shaped to fit comfortably around the lower part of the head.

Towards the end of the first quarter of the fourteenth century a knight could ensure maximum protection. Over his shirt-like undergarment went a padded, long-sleeved *gambeson* or *aketon*; over this was his long-sleeved hauberk with attached mail mittens and quite possibly a raised collar. The hauberk was covered with 'a pair of plates' which was a kind of scale armour with plates riveted to a leather or material garment. Next came the many extras: gutter-like plates to protect the lower and upper arms; discs of metal at the elbows and shoulders; specially shaped plates for the knee and the lower part of the leg. Even the foot now received extra protection in the form of a series of small, overlapping plates. Last to be donned was the bascinet with or without a visor, but almost certainly with a mail curtain or plate defence around its base. The hands were still protected by mail mittens but there was an increasing use of separate gloves (gauntlets) with the fingers covered with small metal scales.

By the second half of the fourteenth century larger plates in the form of steel half-hoops, fastened to some form of garment, were passed round the breast and back. On the Continent, several of these plates were being united to create a larger, single breastplate. Around the middle of this century the arm was given complete plate armour. Two shaped plates now fitted front and back of the arm and were then strapped together while special, overlapping plates guarded the shoulder. Gauntlets were now made of plates with separate finger defences. The leg was also encircled with plates front and back. Although the front of the knee could easily be protected by a shaped plate, the back was more difficult to cover, but the wings of a butterfly-shaped plate (the *poleyn*) curved backwards and slightly inwards to give some protection to this area.

The small, single-plate breastplate served another purpose, for during the last quarter of the

Coment le messager ȝeboun ple
a Abymalech e li counte qe gaıl li
ventoıt prenore e tuer·∶∷∶∶·

Ceo est la bataıle ꝺe Abymalech e
gaıl· E coment Abymalech occıt Gaı
E ganıa la bataıle E entraht en l

fourteenth century a small L-shaped
bracket is occasionally shown
attached to the right side. This was
used in conjunction with the disc
or ring fitted to the lance just behind
the hand grip. When the lance was
couched this disc rested in front
of or touching this L-shaped
bracket. The impact of the lance
hitting something was transferred,
via the bracket, to the breastplate
so that the whole body absorbed
the shock.

Plate armour made it extremely
difficult to strike home with a cut
and the use of thrusting swords
increased. Some knights armed
themselves with a stiff-bladed, thin-
pointed, thrusting sword which
they hung from the saddle, in addition to the broad-bladed, cut-and-
thrust sword which they carried
on the waist-belt. The ordinary

Above:
A vivid battle scene from a Psalter
(book of Psalms), *c.* 1300. The knights
use axes, swords and spears and wear
kettle hats, visored helmets and mail.
Note the plates at the knees.
Queen Mary's Psalter,
British Museum, London.

Right:
This illustration from a late 14th-century
French manuscript shows a favourite
character, St. George, fighting against
the dragon. He wears a pig-faced bascinet
with the visor raised. His body is
protected by a quilted gambeson and his
hands by metal gauntlets.
British Museum, London.

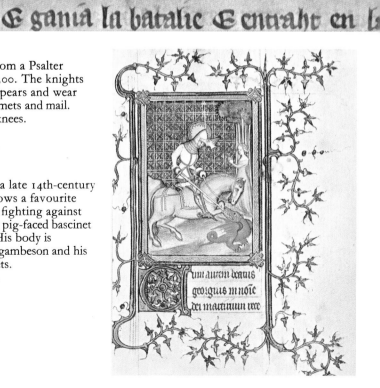

65

Centre:
This harness is from the castle at Churburg in the Tyrol, and is an example of early plate armour with a small, globose breastplate made up of nine pieces. The top of a lance rest can just be seen. The pig-faced bascinet has an applied brass edging and this and the armour dates from *c.* 1390.
Kunsthistorisches Museum, Vienna.

Above:
Large bascinet complete with front plate. The visor is missing but the hinge fitting is there. Small holes around the edge would have held the padding. Late 14th century.
British Museum, London.

Far right:
The mail curtain on the bascinet has here been replaced by plates and except for the armpits and similar vulnerable spots, the defence is entirely of plate. Note the very long shanks to the spurs. (*c.* 1430).

sword usually had a sharp taper to the blade and the quillons were far more down-curved. During the latter part of this century there are indications of new methods of holding the sword. A firmer grip was achieved by hooking the first finger over the quillon. If the blade was sharpened up to the guard then there was a real danger of cutting the finger. To prevent this the top few inches of the blade were often left blunt; this unsharpened section was known as the ricasso.

During much of this century some of the weapons and helmets were fitted with rings through which passed a chain which was, in turn, attached to the belt or the breastplate. These were safety chains to ensure that if a sword or helmet was dropped or struck from the knight's hand, it was not lost, leaving him defenceless. Shortened lances, 5 or 6 feet long, and long-handled axes, often with spikes on the back of the head, were found to be very effective in dealing with the plate armour and these were commonly used. The crossbow was now more powerful and also still very popular.

MONUMENTAL BRASS
of an unknown knight. English, about 1430
Size of original 32" x 9"   5781-1859

The Late Middle Ages

The fifteenth century saw the culmination of the armourers' search and by the first decade the well equipped knight was completely encased in steel. The breastplate covered the whole of the chest and the cuirass was now completed by a backplate. The two sections of the body armour were normally hinged on the left and secured on the right by straps and buckles. The skirt was no longer of mail alone but consisted of strips of metal which overlapped, one above the lower, to form a defence of plates and this too was usually hinged and buckled at the side. The upper and lower arm were now both completely encased and the shoulder was protected by a series of plates (the pauldron) as well as by small discs (besagews) fitted at the armpit. The joints at the elbow and knee still relied, to a certain extent, on mail for their protection. The leg armour was now shaped and covered the thighs and shins while an ingenious arrangement of plates at the knees protected them without limiting their movement. The elbow- and knee-joints usually had a fan or butterfly shaped projection to give some additional protection to the inside of the joint. The feet were protected by overshoes made of small, overlapping plates.

Greatly improved armour meant that it was no longer so necessary to carry a shield which, at the best of times, was an encumberance. However the left side was still rather more vulnerable. On more expensive armours the plates guarding this side were usually a little thicker and sometimes extra reinforcing plates were fitted on the back of the left gauntlet. All these early plate armours have smooth surfaces, the idea being that this would help deflect a blow.

This period saw a tremendous range of helmets; the bascinet was still very much in favour although the old mail curtain had been replaced by a large throat-plate at the

This charming painting of the Battle of Agincourt (1415) does not give an accurate idea of the battle. It does show the use of longbows, by the English; the armour is only sketched in but is faithful in general shape.
Lambeth Palace Library, London.

Left:
William Montagu, Earl of Salisbury, from a copy of the Salisbury Roll, *c.* 1483–85. Although primarily intended to depict heraldic material it gives a good idea of the armour of the period. On the floor are visored sallets. *British Museum, London.*

Right:
A 16th-century German breastplate with roped borders and the roundish form typical of the first part of the century.

Below:
This fine mitten gauntlet has a long cuff and is designed for use in the tilt. It has roped edges to the cuff and plates. German, *c.* 1540.

front. The rear of the bascinet now curved down to overlap the back-plate to which it was secured by a strap and buckle.

The armour, known as a harness, was now so complex that it was almost impossible for a knight to make himself ready for battle un-aided, and a squire or other assist-ant was necessary to help him dress. His basic garment was an arming doublet which went over his vest-like undergarment. The doublet was padded and fitted with a number of leather 'arming laces'. Strips and patches of mail were sewn on the garment at elbows and armpits. He also had a pair of mail drawers and a padded scarf of mail around his neck. His hosen (stock-ings) were padded, especially

around the knees, and he wore small leather shoes. The armour was donned piece by piece starting from the feet and working upwards. First were the foot defences which would be tied on with some of the arming laces. Next came the greaves which were strapped into position. Then came the thigh pieces which were secured by laces and probably tied to a waist-belt. Knee pieces were strapped into place. Next came the body armour which was opened wide, put on and then strapped on the right side and across the shoulders. Next came the plates for upper and lower arm and the elbow pieces which were secured by laces. The shoulder defences, the pauldrons, were simi-larly strapped and laced into

position. Gauntlets were not put on until required and quite often they had a thong so that they could be hitched together and hooked over the hilt of the sword. The helmet would not be put on until action was imminent when this too would be strapped into position. Enclosed in his steel box the knight enjoyed a remarkable degree of freedom and, contrary to common belief, armour was not extremely heavy and limiting. A knight in full harness could perform any movement required: he could lie down, stand up, sit, run, mount and dismount from his horse completely unaided. The idea that the knight was hoisted into his saddle by a crane is an invention of the comic illustrators.

The manufacture of armour was a skilled craft, and was known as a mystery – which it largely remains today. One or two engravings show the inside of an armourers' workshop, but details are scarce. Much of the shaping was done when the metal was cold and the plates were hammered over a metal or wooden stake, but some mechanical power was derived from

SPURS and STIRRUPS
Stirrups were probably first used in China in the fifth century AD. They made a big difference to the cavalry because they enabled the rider to stand in the saddle and so use all his weight for a sword cut or a lance thrust. Spurs are much older and have been used almost since man first rode horses. The earliest were just a U-shaped piece of metal at the back of the ankle with a short spike at the centre; these were called prick spurs. Later in the thirteenth century a rotating, spiked wheel – the rowel – was fitted and the neck had to be longer to reach the flanks of the horse which were then under the armour. In the seventeenth century the neck was angled but later the spurs were straight with a very small rowel.

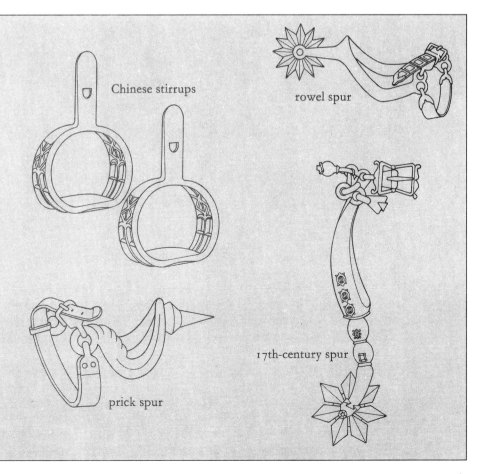

Chinese stirrups

rowel spur

prick spur

17th-century spur

water-wheels. The expertise required to beat the skull of a helmet from one single piece of metal was quite considerable; even today with modern methods and modern tools it is a feat difficult to equal.

The armourer needed certain raw materials: iron ore, coal or charcoal, and some water power was desirable. It is not, therefore, surprising that 'armour towns' developed in areas where these facilities were available and conveniently situated, on or near trade routes. Augsburg, Nuremberg, Passau and Solingen in Germany, Paris in France, and Milan in Italy, all became famous during the Middle Ages for the quality of their armour and weapons. A knight of some means could ensure that he had the very best by sending his personal measurements to an armourer and ordering the very latest style made to measure. Armour was expensive and, for the vain knight, could be covered with material and decorated with precious stones.

Not surprisingly these manufacturing centres tended to develop their own peculiar styles of armour and needless to say each influenced the other. Italian armourers produced a more rounded, smooth appearance with very large shoulder defences which covered not only the shoulder but a good deal of the breast and back as well. The elbow defences were also rather large although still smooth and sweeping in outline. The top of the thigh was given extra protection and a series of plates known as tassets were strapped over the skirt of mail. The wings at the side of the knee and elbow pieces curved nicely round the back of the joint. The cuirass also had a similar

Left:
Soldier on horseback, by Dürer. This 15th-century soldier wears Gothic armour with a visored sallet, but the lower part of the leg remains bare.
Graphische Sammlung Albertina, Vienna.

Right:
Andrea Montegna painted this portrait of St. George, *c.* 1460, and dressed him in Italian armour of the period. It shows the typical rounded shape, tassets and large pauldrons of such armours. Mail still plays an important part in the defences.
Gallerie dell' Accademia, Venice.

Opposite top:
Head of a late 16th-century halberd showing the axehead with spike and cutting edge. The mark of the armourer is stamped into the metal.

Opposite bottom (*from left to right*):
1. 16th-century Corseque from Italy.
2. Late 16th-century Italian bill with traces of decoration on the blade.
3. A form of spiked hammer, 16th century, usually known as a Luzern hammer.
4. Sempach halberd, so called after a battle of that name. This weapon was favoured by the Swiss mercenaries. First half of 16th century.

Below:
Armour for man and horse in the fluted Maximilian style. The horse armour has no side plates (flanchards). German, *c.* 1520.
Tower of London Armouries.

rounded appearance and the breast-plate and back were often made in two or three carefully overlapping pieces which were strapped on the inside, thus giving maximum freedom of movement. The lance rest on the Italian armours was fixed by a series of pierced lugs which engaged with a number of slots on the rest itself, and was then secured by dropping a pin down through the holes. Italian armourers also developed a system of ridges which were carefully placed so that the point of a weapon striking them was guided away from vulnerable points; thus a ridge across the shoulder would help divert a blade from the throat. Again in the interest of comfort, the ends of thigh or shoulder armour were carefully rolled over so as to pro-

duce a smooth rather than a sharp edge. Many English effigies of the period show that Italian armour was popular among the British.

Whilst the Italian armour had a graceful, rounded appearance the German armourers developed a much 'sharper' look. From around the middle to the end of the fifteenth century German armour was spiky and is called 'Gothic'. Breast-plates were usually made of two pieces with a narrow waist, and there was a fairly short skirt of overlapping plates known as the fauld. The surfaces of all the pieces except the greaves were decorated with raised ridges and often when these reached an edge of the plate, the armourer cusped it. The plates were sometimes fitted with a thin layer of brass at the edge as an extra decoration. Arms, shoulders and legs were protected by similarly cusped and ridged plates. The feet were covered with long, pointed metal shoes in imitation of the prevalent civilian styles.

The German armourers produced a style of helmet known as a sallet in which the skull was tapered at the rear to form a pointed tail, sometimes made up of a series of overlapping plates. The sallet was sometimes 'open faced' and sometimes fitted with a visor. These helmets were popular during the late fifteenth and early sixteenth century, and when worn the top of the chest and the throat were protected by a separate plate called the bevor.

Kettle hats, sallets and bascinets were still worn but in the late fifteenth or early sixteenth century a new style of helmet known as the armet was developed. It consisted of a central skull with a long, thin piece which covered the back of the neck. To the side of the upper skull were hinged two cheek pieces, which were raised and then lowered as the skull of the helmet was placed over the head. When the helmet was on, the cheek pieces were strapped into position. They projected forward so that the chin and nose were covered by these side plates and a gap for vision and ventilation was left. Obviously an open space such as this was a point of danger so a small visor,

pivoted on the sides of the skull, could be lowered to complete the covering of the head. Additional protection was added by a separate piece, known as the wrapper, which was secured to the front of the armet by straps which circled the base of the helmet. To give some protection to the straps at the rear of the armet, there was a large, round steel disc.

The armour described above was, of course, expensive and not every knight or soldier would be quite so well equipped. The nobility could afford to have their armour custom built but for the rank and file cheaper, mass produced versions were available and many of the manufacturing towns had a high rate of production. Even the cheaper armours were often ingeniously designed so as to fit almost any size.

Many of the ordinary soldiers called for service would have been lucky to have possessed any armour at all. Although under various statutes many towns, particularly in Britain, were bound to keep a certain amount of armour and military equipment, by no means everyone would have been equipped. After battle, when the sense of relief at surviving was over, one of the first tasks of most soldiers would have been to search around to see what loot, including pieces of armour, could be 'acquired'. Many of the infantry would have been without any armour at all whilst a lucky minority would have had some form of padded or quilted aketon and possibly a brigandine. This was a form of scale armour which had a tunic or shirt covered with small metal plates riveted into place.

It was obvious to the weaponsmith that extra power was necessary to break into the shell of armour and pole-arms, which increased cutting power, became more popular. Axeheads were mounted on shafts of up to six feet long and were frequently fitted with a spike at the top and a hammer-head on the back of the blade. Known as a poleaxe, these weapons proved to be extremely effective: the long shaft gave greater power to the blow. The halberd was

another, powerful pole-arm consisting of an axehead with a spike at the back and a spear-point at the front. The Swiss were particularly adept in the use of this weapon and differing patterns were developed. Both the poleaxe and halberd had the top section of the shaft strengthened with bars of metal known as langets which ran down either side to reduce the chances of the blade being hacked from the shaft. The glaive was a modified spear with a long point the edge of which was sharpened, enabling the weapon to be used both for cutting and thrusting. A shortened version of the poleaxe was designed for cavalry. This was known as the horseman's hammer and it continued in use, particularly in Eastern Europe, until the seventeenth century.

Edged weapons of the fifteenth century were more varied and were often designed with special uses in mind. The mounted knight carried a cut and thrust sword with a long, tapering blade and simple cross quillons. The pommel was normally wheel-shaped, although it could have been pear- or spherical-shaped. The blades were often 'hollow ground', which means they were thick at the centre and thinner towards the edge, so that each half of the blade was faintly triangular. A similar strengthening effect could also be achieved by having a ridge running down the centre of the blade. Some swords, intended for use against armoured opponents, had a long grip, big enough to accommodate both hands for a really hard swing. Estocs (thrusting swords) were still popular and often the section of the blade just below the grip was left blunt so that the blade itself could be gripped and a really vicious thrust made.

The infantry carried swords and from the middle of the fifteenth century there can be seen the beginnings of the very complicated hilts which were fitted to later swords. The quillons of some short, infantry swords were modified so that the rear quillon curved down towards the point whilst the front one curved up and over to touch the pommel. This bar protected the hand when it gripped the hilt and

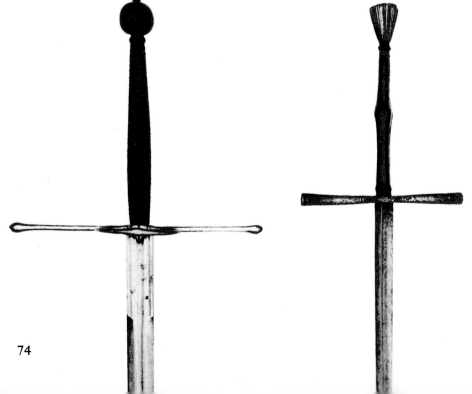

Top right:
Blade of a French partisan pole-arm.
The short side-arms are typical of this
weapon but this one is a little more
ornate than most. The haft is covered
with velvet and has a tassel just below
the blade. Third quarter of 16th century.

Bottom right (*from left to right*):
1. Venetian sword of the 15th century.
The double-edged blade has a single
groove (fuller), the pommel is of an
unusual shape and the quillons are
S-shaped. 45 inches (114.2 cm).
2. German hand and half sword with
long, straight quillons of the 15th
century. These swords had a grip large
enough to be held in both hands if so
desired. 46 inches (116.8 cm).
3. Knight's sword with double-edged
blade and carrying an Arabic inscription.
14th century. 35½ inches (90 cm).

Top left:
This type of breastplate, made up of
overlapping plates, is known as an *anime*.
This example is Italian and dates from
the mid-15th century. The individual
plates are held together by leather
straps.

Bottom left:
Left: German two-handed sword with
straight quillons and ring guards on
each side. First half of 16th century.
61 inches (155 cm).
Right: German thrusting sword (estoc)
with triangular section blade. Quillons
are slightly S-shaped. *c.* 1500. 55 inches
(139.75 cm).

is known as the knuckle bow.
Another development was to
divide the quillon so that one
section was bent down towards the
point and then round and back
again to touch the blade. This
created a ring round the finger
hooked over the quillon and resting
on the ricasso. Additional loops
were fitted at right angles to the
grip, giving extra protection to the
hand.

Skill at arms is not a quality that
most people are born with and a
knight had to undergo a long course
of training. Part of this was taken
up by mock battles. These 'war
games' can be traced back to the old
Roman circus although the form
was rather different. When groups
of knights were involved the events
were called a tourney or tournament
but when only two took part they
were referred to as a joust. The
weapons were normally blunted but

Above:
The Battle of San Romano (1457), by
Uccello. The painting shows many
details of weapons and armour:
horsemen's picks, lances, crossbows,
swords, helmets, mail and crests.
National Gallery, London.

Left:
A matching set of armour for man and
horse, *c.* 1532–36. It is painted black
and the decoration is gilt. The helmet
consisted of a burgonet fitted with a
face-guard – a falling buffe. The total
weight of the man's armour is about
58 lb (26 kg), and that of the horse is
about $61\frac{1}{2}$ lb (28 kg). Both were made
by Hans Ringler of Nuremberg for Otto
Heinrich, the Count Palatine of the
Rhine.
Wallace Collection, London.

Opposite top:
The story of King Arthur was a popular
one and these two illustrations come
from a 15th-century romance about
Lancelot of the Lake, one of the
characters in the Arthurian legends. The
left-hand picture shows a joust with
blunted lances protecting the legs. In the
right-hand picture a knight kneels whilst
his horse, fitted with a chanfron, is
tethered to a tree.
Bibliothèque de l'Arsenal, Paris.

Opposite bottom:
Complete horse armour, *c.* 1500,
probably Flemish. The bard is embossed
with some of the emblems of the Order
of the Golden Fleece.
Tower of London Armouries.

in a *jouste à outrance* normal, lethal weapons were plied with vigour until one knight cried 'Quarter!' or perished. These tournaments became big social occasions and were frequently held in honour of special events such as weddings or coronations. Often they ended in death or injury for the combatants and it was not long before armourers were being asked to provide greater protection. During the fourteenth century the great helm, previously worn in war, which was so big and heavy that its base rested on the shoulders, was largely reserved for these events. Special plates were also fitted to the front of the saddle to give extra protection for the legs.

Early in the fifteenth century an important safety measure was introduced to reduce the chances of the horses colliding and being hurt. A fence, the tilt, was erected down the centre of the field and the contestants took position on either side, with the left-hand side facing the fence. Most jousts were with the lance which was held across the horse's neck and points were awarded for the various hits or for lances broken.

In the sixteenth century another precaution was taken when special forms of tilt armour were developed. Sometimes a complete harness, sometimes just extra pieces fitted to an ordinary harness, this armour consisted of extra plates which were attached by nuts and bolts at the most vulnerable points. In the interests of safety lance heads were rebated (blunted) or fitted with coronels (small, knobbed heads) which would not easily slip off a plate but would not pierce it. Often no gauntlet was worn on the 'lance hand' which was protected by a large, cone-shaped disc, the vamplate, fitted to the lance itself. In the latter part of the fifteenth century a special, hollow lance was used and this *bourdonnasse* was designed to splinter on impact.

Although the majority of courses were fought on horseback, foot combat in the lists was not uncommon and a variety of weapons were used including the lethal poleaxe. Special armours for these

occasions included the tonlet which was a skirt-like defence of hoops.

During the sixteenth century Henry VIII (1509–47), anxious to develop the armour trade in Britain, persuaded some armourers from the Continent to set up a workshop just outside London, at Greenwich by the River Thames. The factory produced some very fine armours both for tilt and war, often etched and engraved, but, in general, only for those people approved of by the king.

Training for the joust and tournament was done in a variety of ways. One of these was the quintain. This had a pivoted arm at one end of which was a wooden shield or a painted face of a Saracen and at the other a weight or a bag of sand. The idea was to ride along at speed, strike the shield and then duck to avoid the weight as it swung round – failure resulted in the rider's being sent spinning from the saddle.

Ironically at the very period when plate armour was reaching its zenith the seeds of its destruction were already being sown. In eleventh-century China, a mixture of yellow sulphur, black charcoal and white saltpetre produced a compound

ANIMALS IN WAR

Unfortunately, man has always involved animals in his fighting. The horse is probably his oldest companion in this respect for it was used from the beginning to carry man to war. Small, wiry ponies helped make the Huns and Red Indians superb light cavalry whilst heavier horses carried the armoured knight into the battlefield.

At first the horse was unprotected, but the Greeks fitted them with some protection in the form of plates to guard the front of the head (*chanfrons*) and the chest (*peytrals*). The Romans also used *peytrals* and *chanfrons*, sometimes decorating them with feathers and crests. During the third century they copied some Persian horsemen and covered their horses with bards or trappers of mail. The trappers were sometimes of scale armour.

Horse armour seems to have been largely discarded between the sixth and the twelfth centuries when mail trappers were re-introduced. From the fourteenth century, plates, either of treated leather or of metal, were used. The horse now had a *chanfron* which sometimes had a spike projecting from the forehead: a *crinet* of plates or mail covered the neck. On the chest was the *peytral*, from the saddle hung two plates called *flanchards*, and the rear of the horse was guarded by a crupper. Horse armour remained in use until the middle of the sixteenth century when it was gradually abandoned, although it lingered on until the middle of the seventeenth century.

In Asia the horse was often armoured with mail or leather and the Japanese fitted it with some large and often grotesque chanfrons. Camels and elephants have been used since ancient times and the latter formed part of the Indian armies until quite recently. A few specimens of armour for these enormous creatures have survived. There are also a few surviving examples of dog armour.

In modern warfare animals are playing a bigger part. Dogs are now trained to locate buried mines, sniff out explosives and drugs, and to find parts of crashed aircraft whose flight detectors have been coated with an extract of human sweat to make them easier to find. Pigeons can now locate and indicate the position of men in hiding, and rats have been trained to sniff out drugs. Dolphins and porpoises, which are highly intelligent animals, now also play a part in warfare: they can be taught not only to identify various warships but also to lay mines alongside them.

horse armour (Milan, 1450)

elephant armour (Battle of Plassey, 1757)

with strange and frightening qualities, known as gunpowder or black powder. At first the Chinese seem to have used it mainly as a psychological weapon, relying on the smoke, flash and roar to surprise the enemy. However, it was not long before the explosive potential was realized and in the twelfth century reinforced bamboo canes were being used as very crude guns. A quantity of the black powder was poured into the tube, which was blocked at one end, and a missile of some sort was rammed in after it. The charge was ignited and it exploded and expelled the missile with some force. How and when knowledge of this powder first reached Europe is unclear. Its existence seems to have been known by the thirteenth century for Roger Bacon, a philosopher and man of science, mentions it in some of his scientific writings. When the first European firearm appeared is not known but there is no doubt that by 1326 the gun was an established weapon in western Europe. In this year the *Milemete Manuscript*, written and illustrated in England, shows a knight igniting a charge of powder contained in a small, vase-like cannon. By a strange coincidence, in the very same year, the records of the city of Florence contain a mention of men being employed to manufacture ammunition and cannons.

The earliest use of gunpowder was by artillery but by the late fourteenth century there are references to handguns. These were comparatively crude, consisting of little more than a socketed iron barrel fitted to the end of a wooden rod called the tiller. The barrel had a small, saucer-shaped depression near the closed, or breech, end and from this a small hole, the touch hole, was drilled through the wall to connect with the central bore. Powder was poured into the barrel, a lead or stone bullet was rammed home and a small pinch of powder was placed in the pan. If a hot iron or a glowing ember was touched to this powder, it flared up and the flash passed through and ignited the main charge to fire the bullet.

These handguns were very inaccurate and probably unreliable

but they heralded the downfall of the armoured knight. At first they were clumsy and awkward to use for they could only be held in one hand whilst the other was igniting the charge but soon a better system, known as the serpentine, was introduced. This was simply a Z-shaped lever, mounted at the side of the tiller: if the lower arm was pressed the upper arm swung forward and down. Into the end of the serpentine was clipped the burning moss or the piece of slow-match. Slow-match was made by soaking a cord of flax or hemp in a strong solution of saltpetre and then allowing it to dry. If the match was lit it burnt very very slowly with a glowing end, ideal for igniting the powder. The long, lower arm of the serpentine was extended back along the stock so that it could be depressed by the hand that held the stock, so giving better control of the weapon. Later this idea was improved and a spring was fitted so

Right:
This miniature shows the Trojan War fought in contemporary costume and arms and armour. The confusion of a medieval battle is well conveyed.
Bibliothèque Nationale, Paris.

Below:
Early 16th-century painting showing the siege of Beauvais. On the left are two early cannons mounted on wheeled carriages.
Musée Archéologique Thomas Dobrée, Nantes.

that once pressure was released the serpentine sprang back clear of the touch hole. This innovation seems to have taken place in the late fourteenth or early fifteenth century.

The next step in the development of firearms was to position the touch hole at the side of the barrel, just above a small, projecting pan which held the priming powder. Barrels were lengthened and the wooden tiller was made in a more convenient shape: thus by the first quarter of the sixteenth century the musket had evolved. It is thought that the name is derived from the Italian word *moschetto*, which means a hawk. It had a long wooden stock which was, by now, shaped so that it could more conveniently fit against the shoulder. The so-called French stock had a very pronounced downward sweep to the butt which seems to have been held against the chest. The Spanish stock was much straighter with the butt drooping only slightly and the end was held against the shoulder. Just to the rear of the breech the waist of the stock was recessed so that it could be firmly gripped with the thumb passing over the top of the stock. In place of the old serpentine lever an internal mechanism, the lock, which was just a simple arrangement of small levers and springs, was now operated by a small movement of a trigger, or tricker. The serpentine holding the match was mounted on a metal plate recessed into the right hand side of the stock. The pan, obviously very much at risk in bad weather, usually had a

pivoted cover which could be swung over the priming powder so as to give some protection against the wind and rain. The serpentine was now fitted at the front end of the lock plate and consisted of a small metal arm which, when the trigger was operated, swung backwards towards the firer, to press the glowing end of the match into the priming powder in the pan.

It was at the breech end that the greatest strength was necessary for it was there that the explosion took place. The breech end of the barrel was thus normally octagonal, gradually becoming circular about a third of the way along its length.

The powder was poured down from the muzzle and was followed by the lead ball which was fairly loose fitting. It weighed some $1\frac{1}{3}$ ounces (12 balls were reckoned to weigh 16 ounces) and was about $\frac{3}{4}$ to 1 inch in diameter. It was essential that the ball should be pushed well down for if a space was left between the powder and the ball dangerous pressures from the explosion could build up. To ram the ball down firmly onto the powder it was essential to have some form of rod. This scouring stick, or ramrod, was housed in a channel cut in the stock beneath the barrel and was used to push the ball down and then returned to its slot.

This matchlock musket was heavy and had a barrel some 48 inches long. Its great virtue was that it required only a minimum of skill to operate. Archers had to practise for hours at the butts to achieve the proficiency needed to win battles; crossbowmen needed expensive equipment and had to undergo training to use this comparatively simple weapon. The musketeer required considerably less skill and training, for provided he could pour down the powder, ram home the ball and press a trigger, all he had to do was to point it in the general direction of the enemy. Provided a sufficient number of these muskets were produced the effect of a volley could be disastrous against even the most heavily armoured troops. Gradually the new firearms began to oust the old, tried weapons and armour, playing a bigger and bigger part in war.

It was quite possible to make armour strong enough to resist the bullet but inevitably it had to be thicker and heavier. Armour had long been subjected to proof which meant that it was stood against a wall or hung on a post and a shot or arrow was fired at it. If the armour was not penetrated it was then described as pistol- or musket-proof. Most of the bullet-dented armour seen today received the damage from this proving process and not in battle. Heavy armour is tiring to wear and was therefore not popular with the troops. If a

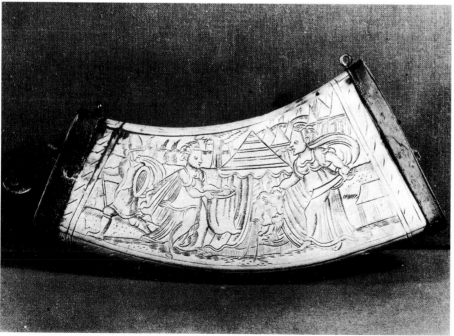

Top:
Butt and lock of a finely decorated matchlock musket, late 16th century. The stock is inlaid and the serpentine is activated not by a trigger but by a lever. Above the breech is a small metal tube which forms the peep-sight.
Nederlands Legeren Wapenmuseum, Leiden.

Bottom:
Body of a powder flask of the late 16th century. The pouring nozzle is missing but the arm to operate the cut-off is clearly visible. Made of cowhorn, the flask is decorated with an engraved picture.
Musée du Berry, Bourges.

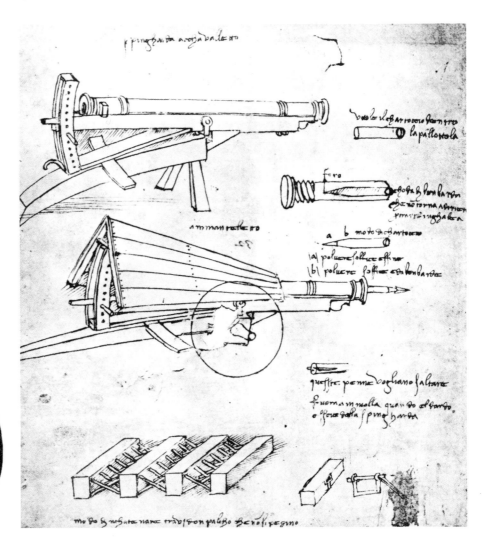

heavy breastplate and helmet had to be worn then often the leg armour was discarded to reduce the total weight carried. This process was emphasized by the change in tactics, for the old, static warfare was changing and a new, fluid, quicker moving style was emerging. This in turn called for troops able to manoeuvre quickly and heavily armoured soldiers found this difficult and tiring so that the process of discarding armour was accelerated.

As a result of the new tactics in warfare, more and more light cavalry were incorporated into the armies. These were troops fitted with three-quarter armours which terminated at the knee leaving the foot and lower part of the leg unprotected except, perhaps, for a strong, leather boot. There were, in addition, some very light horse who fought without any armour at all. Some heavy cavalry were retained until well into the seventeenth century and these were fully armoured from head to foot as were their horses.

The trend towards light armour was also apparent in helmet design. Bascinets, armets and great helms for the tournament were still worn but more popular among the light cavalry was the burgonet. This was a helmet in which the plate visor was discarded or replaced by a defence of bars. Skull and cheek pieces were the same as on many other helmets but above the open front was a forward projecting peak pivoted at the side of the helmet. The face was often protected by some form of bar defence, often attached to the peak. Extra protection was given by the use of a wrapper, a plate which could be fastened to the front of the burgonet leaving just a slit for vision.

The armet was also developed and became the close helm. The skull was made larger and now covered the whole of the back of the head and instead of cheek pieces hinged at the top, a single bevor covered the sides of the face and chin. The bevor was pivoted at the side of the skull as was a visor which, when closed, covered the face except for slits for vision. On many of these helmets the visor could be propped open by means of a hinged bar.

Foot soldiers seldom wore these more elaborate helmets and by the late sixteenth century one of the most common styles was the morion, a name used for two differing patterns. The Spanish form had a cone-shaped skull, often terminating in a little stalk at the top, and a quite narrow brim. The Italian morion was very different and had a wide brim with a roped edge which had a peak back and front and which swept down almost to a point at the centre. Across the top of the skull was a pronounced comb; both often had cheek pieces laced under the chin.

Although the trend was towards the abandoning of armour, this did not mean that there were no developments during this period. On the Continent, particularly in Germany, the fluted, Gothic armour

and the rounded style of the Italian armourers had merged to produce what is known as the Maximilian style. This armour is characterized by the close-set, parallel ridges which covered the surface of the armour except for the lower section of the leg defences, the greaves. The metal shoes were splay-toed imitating the current civilian style known as the 'bear's paw'. The ridges were not purely decorative for they gave extra strength in the same way as do corrugations in iron sheeting. They also served to deflect the point of a weapon away from any vulnerable areas. The edges of almost all the pieces of armour of this style are roped: turned over with an angled depression repeated all the way along the edge.

The Maximilian style remained popular until the 1530s when the ridging began to disappear and almost all armour tended to adopt the smooth surface of the earlier styles. Again civilian fashion affected the design of armour and many of the breastplates from the mid-sixteenth century onwards had a central, raised ridge and a characteristic 'peascod' shape which was the current civilian fashion.

Although the trend was towards lighter armour in battle, on the tourney and tilt field the reverse was the case. Tilt armour was, in the sixteenth century, quite complex. The originally simple concept of a mock battle had developed into a whole range of specialized contests and was now ruled by a series of regulations, and the armours reflected this complexity. It was possible to acquire a basic 'field harness' for war plus a whole garniture of extra pieces which could be attached for the various courses. One of the best known garnitures is that which belonged to Henry VIII and it can be seen in the Tower of London today. It was made at his Greenwich workshop and the basic armour consists of a three-quarter harness with an open-faced burgonet. This could be converted into a field armour with feet and leg defences, a different style of breastplate with a lance rest and two upright collar pieces

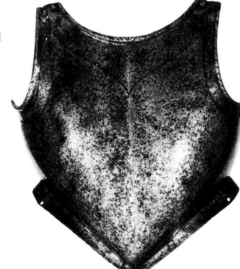

Above:
Very ornately decorated with enamel and embossing, this is an outstanding example of ceremonial or parade armour. The morion retains its earflaps and the plume holder can be seen at the back. The shield and helmet were decorated *en suite* by Pierre Reddon, a goldsmith of Paris, in 1572 for Charles IX of France (1560–1574).
Musée du Louvre, Paris.

Right:
Late 16th-century breastplate with the 'peascod' shape which imitated the civilian style of costume. There are two moveable gussets at the arms to permit just a little extra movement.

Opposite:
Henry IV at the battle of Arques, 1589. The picture is interesting as it illustrates the changing fashions in armour: some of the cavalry wear only a breast- and backplate, whereas others retain full armour. Henry carries a rapier and no pistols are visible.
Palais de Versailles.

known as haute pieces, which were extra protection for the neck and head. The open faced burgonet could be changed into a close helmet by means of a wrapper. For the tilt, where extra protection was needed, a large plate which covered the chest and the left side of the helmet, could be attached to the breastplate. A very large shoulder-guard and upper arm-guard and an extra large gauntlet could also be fitted to the left hand. There were also alternative pieces for foot combat.

Needless to say, this was a very elaborate armour and the majority of the troops were far less well equipped. Units such as the German Landsknechts on the Continent wore a light, three-quarter armour with a very simple helmet and, quite often, a mail cape known as a

bishop's mantle over the shoulders. Around the middle of the sixteenth century a style known as black and white armour was introduced. This was a three-quarter armour which, to protect it against rust, was covered with thick, black paint, except for narrow strips at the edge which were left bright.

During the second quarter of the sixteenth century it became common for civilians to carry a sword as part of their costume. The traditional fighting sword was long and heavy and therefore inconvenient and uncomfortable and consequently lighter forms of sword were popular. The decreasing use of heavy armour meant that swords with heavy blades were no longer needed: longer, lighter blades, primarily for thrusting, were introduced. Armoured gauntlets were

heavy and inconvenient when handling a sword but there was need for some protection for the hand. The developments which started in the late fifteenth century continued until the sword hilt was protected by a basket of loops and bars. During this century many swords became articles of fashion as well as weapons and some very elaborate, ornate and highly decorative sword hilts were produced embellished with chiselling, piercing and inlaid precious metal.

The fighting sword was simpler, usually a double edged cut and thrust blade with a simple cross-guard, usually with a slight downward curve. In Europe, the Swiss were building up a reputation as superb mercenaries, particularly in their use of the devastating halberd and, together with the German

Landsknechts, the two-handed sword. This had a blade some 50 inches long and was nearly 6 feet in length. It was used with both hands. The ricasso was leather covered and this allowed the sword to be gripped at the hilt and on the ricasso so that it could be used as a small lance or spear. Some were fitted with blades which were 'flamboyant' or wavy-edged. The idea was that the angled edge would give a better cut for the same degree of force.

Despite all the changes and improvements to the sword and other edged weapons, the sixteenth century was witnessing the eclipse of the armoured knight, the gallant swordsman, the axe-wielding infantry and the archer. Modern technology was beginning to take over and soon the firearm was to dominate the military scene.

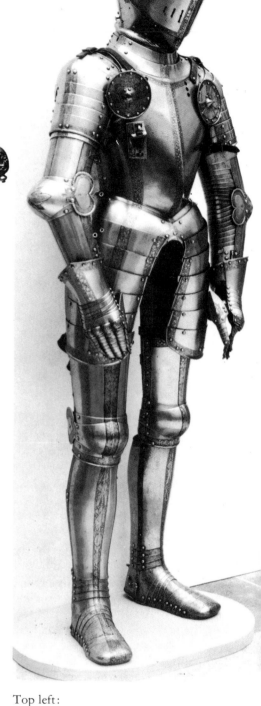

ARMOURER'S MARKS
Armour, swords, daggers and pole-arms frequently carry various marks stamped into them. Some were the armourer's personal mark but most were the view mark of the manufacturing town. The craft of the armourer was usually controlled by a body known as the guild which, in some ways, resembled the modern trade union. If the armour or blade was up to standard it was viewed, approved and stamped with the guild mark which was often part of the coat of arms of the town in which the armour was made. Those of Augsburg and Nuremberg are probably the most common on armour. On swords the famous running wolf is best known and this was used by the blade makers of Passau and Solingen in Germany. On some armours there might be the marks of arsenals or government stores.

Firearms were tested from the seventeenth century and, if satisfactory, stamped with the appropriate mark. In Britain this was a crowned V for the first examination or view and then a crowned G.P. for the final proof. Other towns with proof houses used their own marks.

Augsburg

Nuremberg

Passau and Solingen

Gunmakers' viewmark and proofmarks

Top left:
Superb hilt of a rapier made in Germany late in the 16th century, much of which is decorated with small scenes chiselled in the steel.
Victoria and Albert Museum, London.

Above:
A composite armour, typical of the period, *c.* 1560, made in Augsburg, Germany. It has a close helmet, besagews to protect the armpit as well as vanbraces (arm pieces), with small plates to protect the inside of the elbow.
Wallace Collection, London.

The Seventeenth and Eighteenth Centuries

From early in the seventeenth century there was little doubt as to which direction military technology was taking. Swords, spears, crossbows and even the longbow were still in use but the musket was beginning to dominate the military scene; powder and lead were displacing steel. By the middle of the century most European armies consisted primarily of musketeers with a number of support troops, whilst the 'horse' was essentially light cavalry with just a few fully armoured units.

The gun which was most often used on the battlefield was the matchlock musket. It had a barrel 48 inches long and a wooden stock that was similar in shape to the present-day gun. The large butt was held against the shoulder and the trigger was guarded against accidental discharge by a thin fence or bar of metal, the trigger-guard. One of the drawbacks of the musket was its weight; it was difficult to hold the weapon steady without some support. The musketeer carried a rest which was a stick of ash with a metal U-shaped arm at the top. The ferrule of the rest was pushed into the ground and the matchlock was placed into the U-shaped section, so giving the musketeer some relief from aching arms as well as a steady aiming point.

The musketeer had a choice of loading systems open to him. He could use a horn which contained a quantity of black powder fed out

through a semi-automatic measuring device. The finger was placed over the end of the horn's nozzle and the flask was inverted. A lever was pressed which allowed powder to run out and fill the space between the finger and the cut-off plate inside the nozzle. If the lever was then released the cut-off closed and when the flask was righted a correct

Velasquez's painting of the Surrender of Breda in 1643 shows all the trappings of 17th-century warfare. On the left one man wears a buff coat, often worn as a light form of armour to protect against a sword cut.
Museo del Prado, Madrid.

German crossbow, *c.* 1600. The stock is covered with plaques of horn engraved with military and hunting scenes. The ratchet device – the cranequin – was used to pull back the cord as the bow was too powerful for it to be done by hand.

GRENADES

Clay, glass or wooden containers holding incendiary materials or quicklime to blind an enemy are a very ancient weapon. By the sixteenth century grenades filled with gunpowder were in use and these were about 3 inches in diameter. In the seventeenth century they were hollow, cast iron globes weighing about 2 pounds. A fuse of slow-match was pushed in, lit, whirled around until it was glowing and, at just the right moment, it was thrown at the enemy – if held too long it might explode in the hand, and, if not held long enough, it might be picked up and thrown back. Tall, strong soldiers were chosen to form the Grenadier units which used these weapons. From the middle of the eighteenth century until late in the nineteenth century grenades were rather neglected but during the First World War they made a come-back. Some were thrown by hand but others could be fired from a rifle. Most had some form of fuse which was started before throwing and then burnt for around 5 to 7 seconds. Today there are many kinds of grenades used for many different purposes: tear gas, smoke, signal, blast or fragmentation which split into as many pieces as possible.

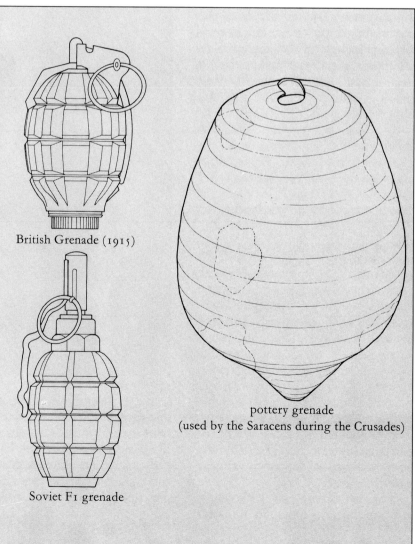

British Grenade (1915)

Soviet F1 grenade

pottery grenade
(used by the Saracens during the Crusades)

charge of powder was held in the nozzle ready to pour down the barrel. The musketeer carried a smaller flask filled with finer grained powder which he used to prime the pan. He could use a paper cartridge which was made from a piece of thickish paper rolled round a wooden former and closed at one end to make a tube into which he placed a charge of powder and one lead bullet. The other end was then screwed up to retain the components. A supply of these cartridges could be carried in some sort of leather box. To load with a cartridge the musketeer bit or tore off one end, poured a small quantity of the powder into the priming pan then tipped the rest down the barrel and dropped the ball, which was still in its paper wrapping, down to follow the powder into the breech. A third method was to use pre-measured charges. Twelve small, wooden, horn or tin flasks were suspended on cords from a broad belt across the musketeer's chest. Each of them held one correct powder charge and when the stopper was removed the contents of the flask were tipped down the barrel, followed by a lead ball which was carried in a bag suspended from the musketeer's belt.

Selection of late 16th and early 17th-century powder flasks as used for wheellock and matchlock weapons. Most were decorated with incised patterns or pictures.

Ifrael ex. cum Priuil Reg.

Ceux qui pour obeir a leur mauuais Genie
Manquent a leur deuoir, vfent de tyrannie,

Ne fe plaifent quau mal violent la raifon;
Et dont les actions pleines de trahifon

Produifent dans le Camp mil fanglans vacarmes
Sont ainfi chaftiez, et paßez par les armes.

12.

This engraving shows a firing squad at work early in the 17th century. The musketeers are using rests – at this range they could hadly miss.

Top:
The hilt of a typical cavalry sword of the middle of the 17th century – the so-called Walloon sword. This example has one of the pierced plates missing from the hilt, although not all examples originally had two fitted. Overall length 42¼ inches (107.3 cm); blade 36¼ inches (92.1 cm).

Bottom:
Hilt of mortuary type sword of early 17th century with a wide, multi-fullered blade. The blade is engraved 'Solingen Clemens Willems Me Fecit'. Solingen in Germany was famous for the production of both armour and blades.
Private collection.

Opposite top:
The hilt of a swept hilt rapier showing the ricasso and the various guards for the hand. The blade is diamond section on this Spanish sword of the very early 17th century. Overall length 43 inches (109.2 cm); blade 37½ inches (96.25 cm).

No matter how proficient the musketeer became he was defence-less whilst reloading. To protect him there were groups of pikemen with spears between 16 and 20 feet long, which could fend off any cavalry attack. The pikemen were still armoured with a cuirass fitted with a very wide metal skirt and a pikeman's pot, which was a kind of morion with a very wide brim. The morion was the only defence worn by the musketeer, who had no other body armour apart from this.

Apart from the pike, pole-arms were now far less used although many ceremonial troops carried a type of partizan or halberd. The seventeenth-century halberd was fitted with an axehead, a very long spear point and a curved spike on the rear of the head. The shafts, particularly those carried by body-guards, were normally octagonal, covered with velvet and decorated with brass-headed studs. On the shaft was a fringe of material which was originally intended to prevent rain running down the shaft and weakening the pikeman's grip.

Both the musketeer and the pike-man may well have carried some sort of sword. This weapon underwent certain changes in the seventeenth century which reflected its diminishing importance on the battlefield and its increasing popularity as an article of fashion. As the century wore on, the lighter, more thrusting sword became more prominent. Earlier on, however, the typical cavalry sword of the English Civil War or the Thirty Years War had a fairly wide, single-edged blade, fitted with a wooden grip bound with wire. The hilt was such that the entire hand fitted into a metal bowl which had been cut and pierced to produce a trellis-like style. The pommel was usually fairly substantial and was, like the basket, often chiselled and decorated. One form of this sword is popularly described as a mortuary sword because of a chiselled head on the basket which is allegedly based upon the death mask of Charles I. A less elaborate weapon is the Walloon sword; this had a double-edged blade, usually convex in section, and a hilt with two pierced plates set at right angles to the blade. A knuckle bow and a small, down-curving rear quillon completed the hand defence. Inside the left hand plate was a thumb ring under which the thumb was hooked to ensure a firm grip.

Late in the sixteenth century there appeared a type of sword which was to become increasingly popular: the rapier, which was also known as the tuck. It was this weapon that was to develop into the small sword, used as a dress weapon. Although some were fitted with a cut-and-thrust blade, it was essentially a thrusting weapon. The earliest form, the so-called Saxon

A page from *The English Military Discipline*, published *c.* 1675, showing the first steps in handling the matchlock. Note the retaining loop at the top of the rest and the method of holding the match. There were numerous instruction books dealing with many aspects of military matters published during the 17th century. *National Army Museum, London.*

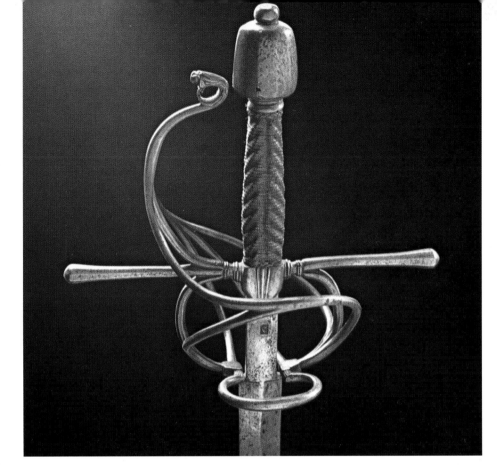

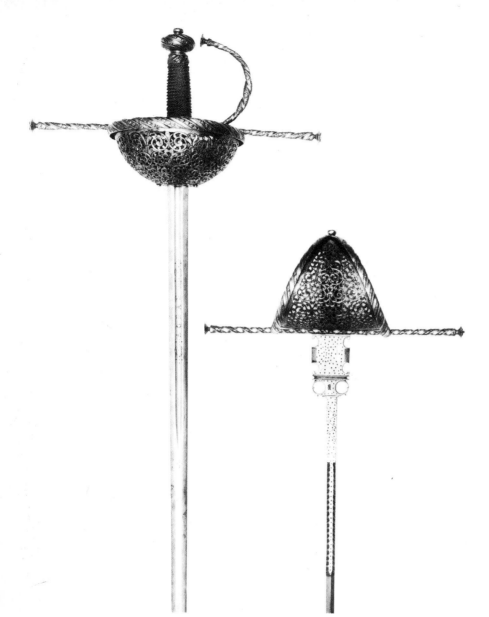

rapier, had straight, flat cross-guards with one or two rings to protect the hand, and a counter-guard to protect the fingers when they were in the ricasso. By the 1570s one of the quillons was turned up to form a knuckle bow. It became increasingly common to sweep bars from the quillons, knuckle bow and counter-guards, so that more and more complex hand guards were formed on the rapier. The next step, which took place from the 1550s, was to fill in some of these rings with a pierced plate. Early in the seventeenth century these small plates began to replace more of the bars on the swept hilt rapier. The earliest were fairly small and situated at the base of the rings; from early in the seventeenth century, however, this idea was developed and the plates were made larger.

One form of rapier that used bars and plates in the hilt was the Pappenheimer. It appeared around the 1620s and the name suggests that it was an attempt to honour one of the leading figures in the Thirty Years War: Field Marshal Gottfried Heinrich Graf von Pappenheimer. The blade was generally rather longer and broader than the usual rapier and had shells which were large enough to replace many of the bars.

The logical extension of the concept of bars and baskets to protect the hand was to unite them into a single metal cup and during the first quarter of the seventeenth century the cup-hilt rapier appears. At first the cup was not quite complete, only becoming so during the second quarter of the seventeenth century. In Spain and areas under her influence such as Italy,

the cups were often beautifully chiselled and pierced. The pommel is often decorated 'en suite' with the cup. The thin knuckle bow swept up in a rather graceful curve from the inside of the cup to the pommel. Two thin, straight quillons extended beyond the cup, inside which two further bars formed the arms of the hilt. The index and second finger were looped through these two arms.

The cup-hilt rapier, although it captured the imagination of illustrators and actors, had a somewhat limited period of popularity although plainer versions were made in Spain until well into the eighteenth century.

One example of civilian use of weapons is the art of fencing. By the middle of the sixteenth century this had become highly complex and sometimes utilized both sword

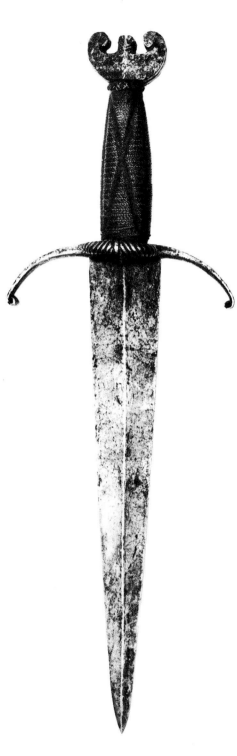

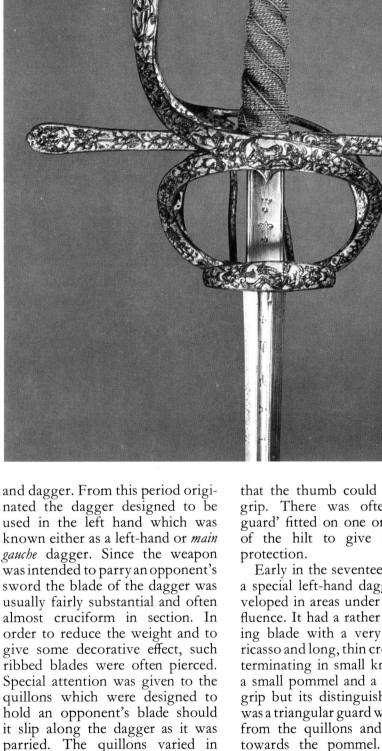

Above:
Italian left-hand dagger with broad blade, thin quillons and single-ring guard. 16 inches (41 cm). Mid-16th century.

Right:
The hilt of the swept hilt rapier was chiselled and gilt by an outstanding craftsman, Daniel Sadeler of Munich, some time early in the 17th century. The swordsmith's marks can be seen stamped on the ricasso.
Victoria and Albert Museum, London.

and dagger. From this period originated the dagger designed to be used in the left hand which was known either as a left-hand or *main gauche* dagger. Since the weapon was intended to parry an opponent's sword the blade of the dagger was usually fairly substantial and often almost cruciform in section. In order to reduce the weight and to give some decorative effect, such ribbed blades were often pierced. Special attention was given to the quillons which were designed to hold an opponent's blade should it slip along the dagger as it was parried. The quillons varied in shape and design but they usually curved down and rose slightly so that they did not lie quite parallel with the blade. So that the dagger could be held firmly there was quite often a small, saucer-like depression in the ricasso to ensure that the thumb could get a good grip. There was often a 'ring-guard' fitted on one or both sides of the hilt to give some extra protection.

Early in the seventeenth century a special left-hand dagger was developed in areas under Spanish influence. It had a rather thin, tapering blade with a very broad, flat ricasso and long, thin cross-quillons terminating in small knobs. It had a small pommel and a wire bound grip but its distinguishing feature was a triangular guard which sprang from the quillons and curved up towards the pommel. This *main gauche* was often supplied with a matching rapier both decorated *en suite*. A few left-hand daggers were produced with very elaborate blades designed not only to parry an opponent's blade but also to hold it and possibly, with a smart twist

Above:
This basket hilt is pierced and decorated with applied silver decoration. The blade is marked 'Me Fecit Hunslo' which means that it was made at the English factory in Hounslow, just outside London, in the latter part of the 17th century.
Victoria and Albert Museum, London.

Opposite top:
Silver hilted smallswords.
From top to bottom:
1. English with triangular blade and hallmarked for 1756.
2. English, London hallmark for 1724. The blade is triangular with spiral fluting on the hilt. 40 inches (101.6 cm).
3. German mid-18th century. The blade has some traces of gold decoration. 35 inches (88.9 cm).

Opposite bottom:
Hunting trousse or sword with knives and file used for dismembering the kill. The set is dated 1662 and the hilts are decorated *en suite*.

or wrench, even to break it. Some left-hand daggers had a blade so deeply notched that the weapon becomes more of a comb-shaped device to snag the opponent's blade.

Another dagger of the seventeenth century was the gunner's *stilletto* or stylet which seems to date back to late in the sixteenth century although the majority of surviving examples are of seventeenth century origin. They had a long thin blade, a smallish grip and very short quillons, no more than a couple of inches across. These daggers often served as a ready reckoner to assist the artillerist in calculating the charge of powder, and on many the sturdy, triangular blade is marked with a series of lines and numbers. Unfortunately, it is

not known how these figures were used.

The habit of carrying a dagger at the belt died out during the seventeenth century but one type was still worn: the ballock dagger. This type had been used from the late thirteenth or early fourteenth century and it seems to have been particularly popular in northern Europe. The people of the Tudor and Stuart period, who did not share the prudery of later eras, chose this name because of the very phallic shape of the handle. It was usually of boxwood and had a long, tubular grip with two rounded lobes as quillons.

The ballock dagger probably served as a pattern for the Scottish dirk whose hilt originally had the characteristic shape with the two small rounded lobes. These were later increased in size and extended further up the hilt and in the eighteenth century the shape of the hilt was far more bulbous. The shape of the early dirk blades suggest that they were originally the ends of sword blades, and the tradition was maintained with the blades being manufactured to suggest the original shape with a single edge and the first few inches given a false edge. Dirks from the eighteenth century onwards usually have the wooden grip decorated with a complicated, Celtic, woven pattern. The sheaths for these dirks were originally fairly plain but during the eighteenth century there was a tendency to fit extra pockets to hold a knife and fork. Following the Jacobite rebellion of 1745–46, Scottish culture was very much frowned on and laws were passed forbidding the use and wearing of all things Scottish. Tempers and memories cooled, however, and in 1782 these laws were repealed and many Scottish traditions were exaggerated in reaction. The dirk, which by then had largely ceased to be a weapon, became even more decorative with large pieces of mineral fitted on the pommel.

As the seventeenth century progressed, the sword replaced the dagger as the principal dress weapon. The great length of the earlier rapiers was seen to be self-defeating for, although it offered a long reach, the sheer size of the blade made it difficult to handle. Thus during the early part of the seventeenth century swords became shorter. The Pappenheimer was rather too military and perhaps a little too sturdy for town wear and so lighter and more elegant rapiers were produced; the dish rapier of the second quarter of the seventeenth century was fairly light with a very shallow dish which was little more than a circular plate.

From the middle of the seventeenth century rapiers gradually became obsolete and a newer, more decorative light sword, known as the small-sword, began to develop. It was the desire for a light sword for everyday wear that led, probably in France during the late sixteenth century, to the production of a sword which was almost a miniature rapier, complete with guard, metal shell, quillons and knuckle bow. These earlier small-swords were fitted with a double shell-guard, a cross-quillon and two arms of the hilt. A knuckle bow was added and the shells began to differ in size. The small-sword of the seventeenth century is far heavier than the later versions which were very delicate and light, seldom weighing more than a few ounces. From about the middle of the seventeenth century the hilt changed very little in general shape although quite considerably in detail. The small-swords of the late eighteenth century have only traces of the original arms of the hilt. As the old style of holding the sword with the index and second finger through the arms of the loop went out of fashion, so the need for the arms of the hilt disappeared. Shells changed for whereas on the earlier swords there is often a difference in size from left to right, on the later swords these become smaller and almost equal. There were differences in the blades, the most common being probably the straight blade with an oval section; the edge was seldom sharpened for it was essentially a thrusting weapon.

The earlier swords had *coliche-marde* blades which were wide for the first third of their length and then abruptly tapered to a very

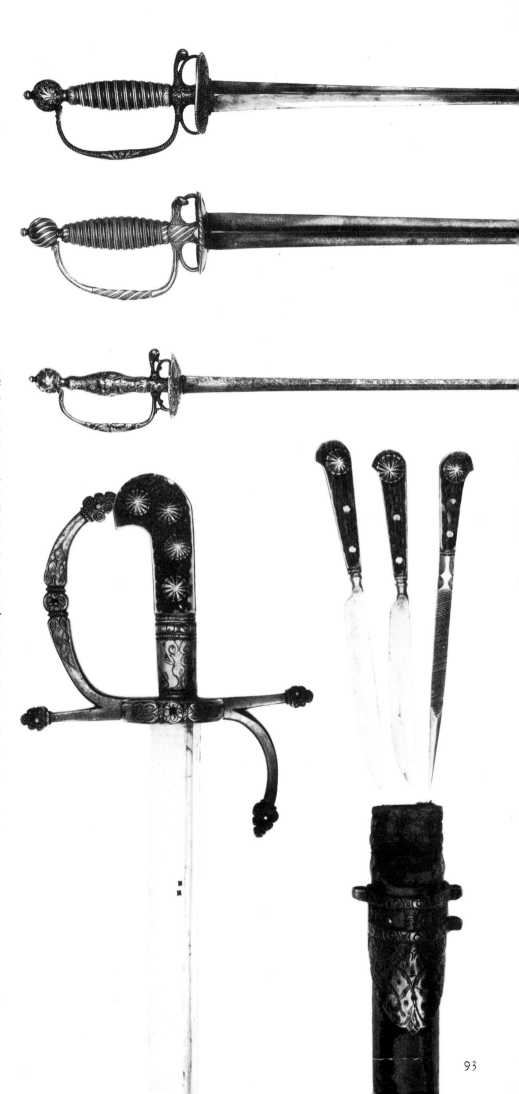

Left:
Hilt of a very fine quality *schiovana*, which was a sword used by mercenaries employed by Venice during the late 17th and early 18th century. The pommel is inset with semi-precious stones.
Private collection.

Below:
English plug bayonet with the mark of the London Cutlers' Company on the blade. The grip is carved with a twist pattern and the quillons terminate in heads. Late 17th century. $17\frac{1}{2}$ inches (44.5 cm).

Opposite:
The armour of James II of England (1685–88). The face-guard of the burgonet is fashioned in the shape of the royal coat of arms and the breastplate and helmet are decorated, as is the bridle gauntlet worn on the left hand. The buff coat was usual wear for cavalry at this period.

narrow section. Since the majority of the opponents' cuts would be taken on the top part of the blade this section was wide and strong, but to allow for swift, thrusting movements and for being able to slip round an opponent's guard, the rest was slim. The name Coliche-marde is derived from that of John Philip Count von Konigsmark, a Swede who became a Marshal of France. This type of blade appeared late in the seventeenth century and went out of fashion around the first quarter of the eighteenth. Another type of blade was known as hollowground and was triangular in section to give great rigidity and extreme lightness.

The adoption and general use of a light, thrusting type of sword which could not give such a good cut at armour, emphasizes the fact that by the beginning of the eighteenth century armour had virtually disappeared from the battlefield. A few cavalry units retained their breast- and backplates and some cavalry officers wore a padded, metal skull cap beneath their broad brimmed, felt hats to give protection against the slash of a sword.

The rate at which armour was discarded was accelerated as fire-arms became more plentiful and new systems of ignition made them more efficient. The old matchlock musket in use in the seventeenth century could be produced and repaired by virtually any competent blacksmith and required little skill to handle it and in consequence was available in bulk for the infantry.

For cavalry it was different and the problems involved in handling a long, heavy musket on horseback – trying to cope with a piece of match which had to be kept aglow while managing a spirited horse or delivering an attack – made it impossible for the cavalry to be equipped with matchlock weapons. If the cavalry was to be armed and the matchlock was to be freed from its very severe limitations then alternative, mechanical methods of ignition were essential.

The first indication of a different system appeared early in the sixteenth century and Leonardo da Vinci is known to have experimented with a mechanical system of ignition: by 1510–20 firearms using a new method are frequently mentioned in contemporary documents.

The outcome of these early experiments was the wheellock, where the burning match was replaced with an ingenious, mechanical spark-making device. A small, steel wheel with an edge grooved and roughened was made, by springs, to rotate against a piece of naturally occurring mineral, known as pyrites. The friction between the two produced small, incandescent sparks and as the wheel was situated at the base of the priming pan and the pyrites touched the wheel through the priming powder, sparks were released immediately into the priming and the shot was discharged. This new system had several virtues. Firstly it avoided the problem of keeping a piece of

94

match burning. Secondly, a weapon fitted with it could be made ready for firing and left with reasonable safety, which was impossible with the matchlock. Thirdly, and very important, it could be made in a range of sizes: large to fit onto a musket, or very small to fit onto a smaller firearm such as the pistol. Pistols probably derive their name from Pistoia in Italy and the appearance of these weapons was a very important step in the story of firearms. Now, for the first time, cavalry could conveniently be equipped with firearms.

There were, however, snags with the wheellock. It was mechanically complex and beyond the capability of any but the skilled metal worker; it was also more likely to be jammed or broken. This meant that it was expensive to produce and perhaps a little less reliable than the sturdy, simple matchlock. Cost alone was a restricting factor and, in general, the wheellock pistol of the sixteenth century was limited to a few cavalry units and ceremonial bodyguards. It was issued on a wider scale during the seventeenth century when far simpler, plainer versions were produced. Wheel-lock rifles were common during the latter part of the sixteenth and for most of the seventeenth century but they were usually the property of people who could afford to pay for top quality work. Consequently most of these wheellock rifles, intended for hunting or sport, were decorated with inlaid wood, horn, ivory and chiselled steel.

Wheellock pistols of the late sixteenth century were often ornate with acutely angled butts with a large ball pommel. The ball was not intended for use as a club but was merely a convenient means of drawing the pistol from the holster. It was either hollow or made of very light wood and as most of these pistols were decorated with inlay, few owners were likely to damage their prize pistol by hitting somebody with it. The cavalry units that were armed with wheellocks carried two in holsters at the front of the saddle.

Wheellock and matchlock firearms suffered from the same handicap in that they had to be reloaded

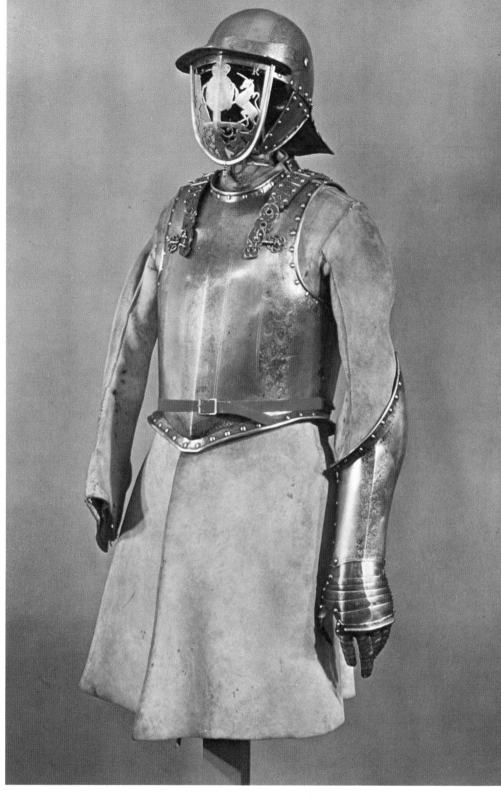

for each shot. Attempts were made early on to overcome this problem, but with the matchlock musket no really satisfactory solution was produced, although a few were made with a group of barrels that rotated so that each would be fired in turn. The wheellock simplified matters and often two barrels were mounted one above the other on a central block and each connected by a touch hole to a separate lock. Another system that was far more hazardous was the superimposed

load. This required only one barrel with two or more touch holes and some special means of priming and firing at each hole. A charge of powder and ball were poured down the barrel, and a thick wad of pressed card, felt or similar material was then pushed home above this charge. A second charge of powder and another ball were then poured in on top which was again wadded to hold it in place. The lock was arranged so that the front load was discharged first, while the wad

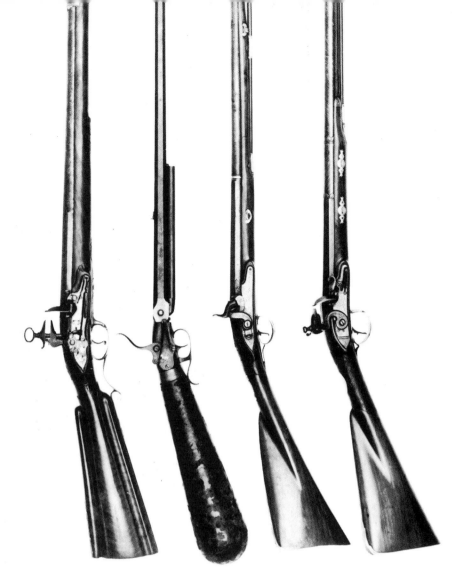

prevented the explosion triggering the rear charge, which could then be fired separately. One cannot help feeling that a certain element of risk attended its use!

The wheellock pistols lasted through the sixteenth century and up to the middle of the seventeenth, by which time it was becoming obsolete. It proved fairly reliable, but gunsmiths were already looking for simpler, cheaper systems. The answer came from a French gunmaker named Marin le Bourgeoys who produced the first workable models during the first decade of the seventeenth century. He took certain basic ideas from other people and combined them to create a simple, efficient mechanism. Early in the sixteenth century there are references to locks which struck sparks between steel and flint: this was the basis of Le Bourgeoys' system. A wedge-shaped piece of flint was gripped between the jaws of a mechanically propelled arm. When the trigger was pressed this arm moved for-

ward to swing the flint through an arc. The edge of the flint was so positioned that it rubbed down the surface of a flat, steel plate producing minute sparks of incandescent steel, and these sparks dropped into the priming powder. This was to form the basis of the ignition method for firearms, both pistol and long arm, for the next 140 years.

The typical French lock of this period consisted of a metal plate let into the side of the firearm. On the outside was a graceful S-shaped arm, known as the cock, which held the piece of flint between two adjustable jaws. The priming pan was also an integral part of the lock plate. To prevent priming powder being lost in the wind or dampened by rain, it was covered by a metal plate. This pan cover was attached to the steel face which produced the sparks. This L-shaped piece of metal – the frizzen – was held down over the pan by means of a small V-shaped spring, known as the frizzen spring. The cock was pulled back as far as it would go

and then locked into place by a small metal arm on the inside of the lock. When the trigger was pressed the arm was disengaged and under pressure of the large V-spring the arm swung forward. The flint scraped down the steel – making sparks and at the same time tilted the frizzen clear of the priming pan, allowing the sparks to drop into the priming and so fire the pistol.

The internal mechanism was far simpler than that of the wheellock and, on the whole, it was more reliable. It was certainly cheaper to produce and simpler to maintain. There was a safety position for the cock so that the pistol could be carried loaded and primed. Despite these inherent advantages it was not immediately accepted and seems to have been used only by French gunmakers for the first 20 or 30 years of its life. By the middle of the seventeenth century, however, it was more widely used and had soon displaced other systems. Armies were gradually re-equipped with the new flintlock musket and

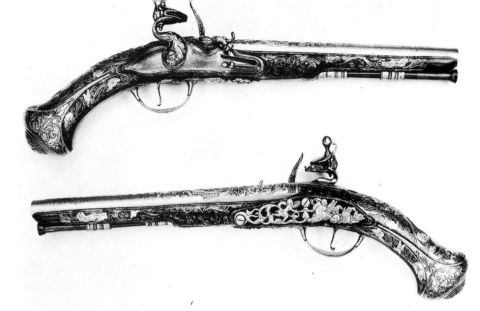

in some cases a flintlock was fitted in place of the old matchlock; a few weapons had both types of lock.

In earlier times the musketeer had been protected by the pikemen but by the latter part of the seventeenth century few of these were still in service. To defend themselves when their musket was empty troops had a new weapon, the bayonet, which converted the musket into a pike. The bayonet derived its name from the French town of Bayonne which was famous for its production of hunting knives. It was a short, dagger-like weapon with a straight blade which tapered rather sharply, a flat cross-guard and a turned wooden handle which narrowed towards the pommel. This bayonet, carried in a small leather sheath at the belt, could be rammed down the muzzle so converting the musket into a 6-feet pike which would hold off cavalry and keep an attacker at his distance. The limitation of this weapon, known as the plug bayonet, was that once in position the musket was useless as a firearm. A variety of systems to circumvent this problem were tried and the most satisfactory was the socket bayonet. This had a short tube of a diameter sufficient to fit over the outside of the muzzle and on one side of this tube was a small, curved arm which terminated in a blade of some 18 inches to 2 feet in length. As the muzzle was now left clear the musket could still be fired even with the bayonet in position, should the need arise.

Although the pike had disappeared from the battlefield it was not the end of pole-arms altogether. In the British army NCOs and officers still had the spontoon which was a short pole-arm carried more as a badge of rank than as a serious weapon. It was discarded by British officers in 1786 and by the NCOs in 1830. It had a flat head with two side points rather like a flattened trident.

By the eighteenth century every European army had most of its infantry equipped with a flintlock musket and a bayonet and the cavalry with a sword and a pair of pistols. Some of the cavalry were

FIREARM ACCESSORIES

As firearms became more complex so they require more and more extra items. Pocket flintlocks were loaded by unscrewing the barrel and for this barrel keys were necessary. Some slipped over the barrel and engaged with a lug, others were pushed into the muzzle to lock into notches. When the percussion system was invented a special key for undoing the nipple was introduced and this was also made to serve as a screwdriver. Various clamps to hold the springs when stripping the lock were necessary and these were sometimes included in a cased set. Small metal oil bottles and ivory boxes for holding spare nipples were another feature of cased percussion weapons.

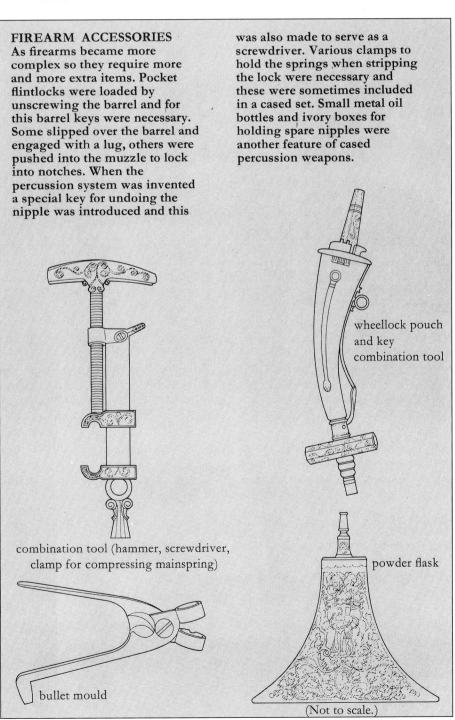

wheellock pouch and key combination tool

combination tool (hammer, screwdriver, clamp for compressing mainspring)

bullet mould

powder flask

(Not to scale.)

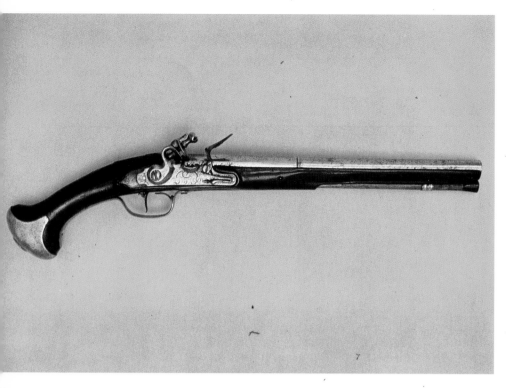

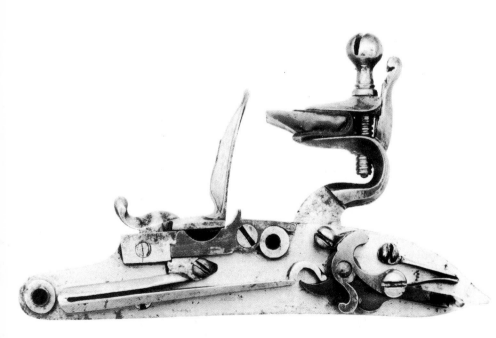

Top:
Fine early flintlock pistol by Gille Penel of Paris, c. 1640. It has a belt hook and a steel butt cap. Overall length 19½ inches (49.5 cm). Barrel 12 inches (30.5 cm). *P. Murray Collection.*

Centre:
Flintlock pistol by Mathias Bramhafer of Augsburg. Each barrel has its own steel and pan but there is only one cock. The butt terminates in a birds-head pommel.
The Metropolitan Museum of Art, New York. Gift of Gustave Diderrich, 1937.

Bottom:
The inside view of a detached flintlock showing the fairly simple mechanical arrangements in contrast to the rather complex wheellock.
Private collection.

Opposite:
Back and front plates of a French gorget of the early 17th century. It is embossed with Classical scenes.
Victoria and Albert Museum, London.

also equipped with a carbine which, like the old caliver, was a shorter, lighter version of the musket. The infantry and most of the officers still carried a sword as part of their standard equipment and in the British army these were not withdrawn from the troops until 1768. Scottish troops were allowed to retain their characteristic sword known as the claymore. The true claymore, the original great sword, *claidheamh mór*, was a large, two-handed weapon with a broad blade and acutely angled, down-sweeping quillons, ending in a pierced quatre-foil. These had been carried in Scotland from the sixteenth century and during the seventeenth century extra protection to the hand was given by a large plate situated at the centre of the quillons. This was the true claymore but the name had been increasingly applied to the basket-hilted Scottish sword. This was a double-edged sword, the hilt of which was a quite complex, pierced metal basket. The Scottish claymore with its large, steel basket hilt, is still carried today on cere-monial occasions by many Scottish troops.

The flintlock musket adopted by the British Army in the 1720s is known as the Brown Bess. It was a simple, well made musket and throughout its hundred or more years of active service was produced in a variety of styles. The early types had a 46-inch barrel which was subsequently reduced to 42 inches and later, under pressure of production problems during the Napoleonic wars, to 39 inches, only to be replaced by the last model which had a 42-inch barrel. Brown Bess had a large, conventional flintlock and a walnut stock of simple but very pleasing outline.

The French equivalent was the model of 1763 and there were two main differences between the two muskets. The first was that the French bullet was slightly smaller. The second was the method of attaching the barrel to the stock: the French, like most of the Continental smiths, did this by means of loops which encircled both and were held in place with a screw. The end of the stock near the muzzle had quite a substantial nose band. The English fitting was far more complex with a series of lugs welded on the underside of the barrel which engaged with corresponding slots on the stock and were then held in place by pins.

Flintlock pistols were produced in a great variety of forms, supplying the civilian as well as the soldier. There were small ones for the lady or the gentleman to carry in their pocket or purse, larger versions to be carried in an overcoat and the long barrelled ones which were used by cavalry. There were graceful pocket pistols in the Queen Anne style, with inlaid silver wire decorations and long side spurs to the butt cap. Many of these 'civilian' pistols had a centrally mounted flintlock which was preferred by gunmakers for pocket pistols. It reduced the size as well as the possibility of sharp edges snagging onto pockets and preventing a 'quick draw'.

A great variety of systems to overcome the 'single shot' limitation were tried, including the tap action whereby an upper and lower barrel were fired successively by turning a bar at the side. There were the superimposed load weapons as well as some flintlocks which had magazines for powder and ball situated in the butt of the stock so that the weapon could be loaded several times from one filling, thus

becoming a repeating flintlock. There were pistols with many barrels (up to five). All these weapons, however, suffered from limitations of varying degrees.

One big disadvantage of most flintlock weapons was their inaccuracy but this was more the fault of the barrel than the construction of the lock. When a musket or pistol with a smooth bore was loaded, the ball did not fit very tightly. As the powder was fired and the ball moved forward it tended to bounce along the inside of the barrel. The amount of 'bounce' was very small indeed but, nevertheless, the ball did swing from side to side in the barrel. As it left the muzzle it was pure chance as to which side or which part of the surface of the ball was last in contact with the inside of the barrel. This contact would always tend to throw the ball

very slightly one way or the other and the throw would never be in exactly the same direction. When this tiny variation was projected over some 50 yards, the deflection was considerable. There were also variations in the charge of powder, the quality of powder, the speed at which the powder burnt, the size, shape and weight of the ball: all these factors affected the accuracy. This inaccuracy was of minor importance in a battle because volley fire was used and a percentage of hits was all that was expected and required.

If the differences in points of contact as the ball left the muzzle could be controlled and made constant, then obviously the ball would always fly in the same direction. If variations caused by imperfections in the cast bullet could be controlled or cancelled out, then

Brass barrelled blunderbuss pistol by the famous London gunmaker, Henry Nock. Late 18th century.

again there would be an improvement in accuracy. The answer, which had been known from the beginning, was to spin the ball. If this could be done there was a gyroscopic effect which would tend to keep the projectile on a steady course and any wobbles due to an irregularity on the ball would be cancelled out by the spin since the effect would be spread through 360 degrees. Rifling was the means by which this spinning could be achieved and the secret lay in spiral cuts on the inside surface of the barrel. These cuts were produced in a great variety of styles: some were deep, some were shallow, some were wide, some were narrow; the number varied from two up to twenty or thirty. All had the same object which was to grip the bullet very tightly and to turn it as it travelled along the barrel, so that when it left the gun at the muzzle it was spinning. The big problem was the purely mechanical difficulty of cutting the spiral grooves. It could be done but only with difficulty and consequently rifles (weapons with rifled barrels) were never issued on a large scale before the middle of the

nineteenth century, although the technique had been established in the seventeenth.

A number of units from various European armies were issued with rifles at different periods, but it was not until the American War of Independence (1775–83) that the rifle gained a reputation as a serious military weapon. It is often believed that the rifle played a major part in this war; this was in fact a fallacy as the majority of American troops were armed with a smooth bore musket in the same way as the British, the French and the Hessian troops. A number of the American units, particularly the militia and volunteer units, were armed with long barrelled, small bore rifles, the so-called Kentucky or Pennsylvanian long rifles. The long barrel ensured a maximum velocity for a given charge of powder and the small bore meant that a smaller bullet was used so that velocity could be maintained and the trajectory better controlled. Above all, use of rifling techniques gave an accuracy largely unknown to the Brown Bess, and there are numerous contemporary stories of the remarkable accuracy of these American rifles. Despite the obvious advantage rifles were still not universally accepted by any of the European armies for some time yet.

By the close of the eighteenth century only lingering traces of the old, armoured knight were still to be found on the battlefield. The only piece of armour – if such it could be called – still used by the majority of forces was the gorget. This was a small, crescent-shaped piece of metal of either silver, gilt or brass, worn at the throat by officers solely as a badge of rank. Originally it had been a piece of armour fitted to the bottom of a helmet or worn as a separate plate but during the seventeenth century when armour was discarded, this piece had for some reason lingered on. It became ornamental rather than functional and was made smaller and engraved with the Royal Coat of Arms or the regimental number. The British abandoned it in 1830. One or two units still retained their breast- and backplate in the case of the cavalry, but these were few and far between. The sword had been discarded by most of the infantry but was still carried by the cavalry and the bayonet had replaced the sword and dagger. War was becoming more and more a matter of fire power and victory was increasingly affected by the industrial might of the campaigning nations who were now able to mass produce cheap, efficient and identical weapons.

The Nineteenth Century

The nineteenth century saw the introduction of the products of industrialization into warfare. For the first time manufacturers had at their disposal machines which were capable of turning out large quantities of virtually identical products. The new skill of the mechanical engineer made it possible to produce equipment cheaply and accurately at a rate which would have been impossible in the previous century. Science was also advancing at a rapid rate and new discoveries were pressed into service by the military technicians, especially in the field of firearms.

When the nineteenth century began Europe was at war. France and England, each supported by various allies, were the main protagonists. Their equipment varied in detail but was essentially the same. All were armed with flintlock weapons and by now the system of regulation issues of firearms was usual with most of the western nations. Thus although the details varied most countries had adopted a system whereby a pattern would be decided on for a weapon which would then be produced in state manufactories or by private contractors working to a sample model. Most countries had an established arms industry. In Britain this was largely concentrated in London and Birmingham; in France a number of arsenals had been set up at places such as St Etienne and Charleville. In the United States, during the War of

Independence, two national arsenals had been set up at Harper's Ferry and at Springfield.

The sword was probably the weapon that varied the most, and throughout the whole of the nineteenth century and spilling over into the twentieth, there was a great debate as to which was the better sword for the cavalry. Some preferred a long, stiff-bladed, thrusting sword, others championed a curved, broad-bladed, single-edged, slashing sword, while yet others sought some effective com-

The lance was re-introduced to Europe by Napoleon, but in the East it had always been popular. Many Indian regiments used it, for example the Skinners Horse, who are shown here practising by spearing tent pegs. Painting by J. R. Giratkin, 1840. *National Army Museum, London.*

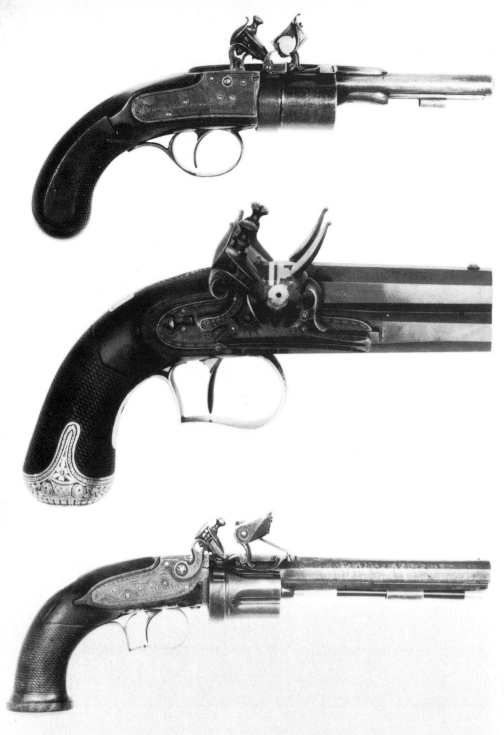

Top:
Flintlock revolver by Elisha Collier.
This is the earlier model with a plain
cylinder. It is also fitted with an auto-
matic priming magazine. *c.* 1820.
Victoria and Albert Museum, London.

Centre:
Fine double-barrelled, over and under
flintlock pocket pistol by Joseph Egg, a
famous gunmaker of Piccadilly, London.
It has all the refinements such as a
platinum touch-hole to resist corrosion.
C. 1820. 6 inches (15.24 cm).

Bottom:
Flintlock revolver by Elisha Collier
with automatic priming magazine. This
is the second version with a fluted
cylinder.
Victoria and Albert Museum, London.

promise. The question was never
really settled until the beginning of
the twentieth century when the
British produced a very fine cavalry
thrusting sword; by then however,
the cavalry were long out of date
and the question was largely aca-
demic. Napoleon's *cuirassiers*, the
heavy cavalry, favoured a long,
stiff sword with a basket hilt whilst
the British heavy cavalry had a
broad-bladed sword which lacked
the strengthening ridges of the
French sword, and which had a
steel knuckle bow and plate defence
for the hand. Light cavalry on both
sides favoured curved swords and
probably the best British sword was
the 1796 Pattern, a broad, single-

edged, curved blade with a plain
stirrup hilt. The standard sword for
the infantry officer had also been
formalized and was a sturdier
version of the civilian small sword
with a long, tapering blade, a hilt
which consisted of two side shells,
a knuckle bow and a small rear-
projecting quillon and a wire-
bound grip.

Most of the military swords
carried from the middle or earlier
part of the eighteenth century had
a sword knot attached. This was a
loop, usually of leather, which was
fixed to the hilt of the sword and
through which the right hand was
slipped before grasping the hilt. It
was, in a way, a modern version of
the old chained helmet and sword
of the knight, for should the sword
be knocked from the hand, it only
dangled from the wrist and was not
lost. Most scabbards were of leather
although steel ones were becoming
more common. Metal scabbards
might be more practical as they
were tougher and harder wearing,
but they could damage the sharp
edge of the sword unless the blade
was withdrawn with care so that
the edge did not rub against the
lip of the scabbard.

Pole-arms had largely disappeared but there was a return to
one weapon long absent from the
battlefields of Europe: the lance.
When Napoleon fought his campaigns in eastern Europe he had
been very impressed with the dash
and effectiveness of the Polish
lancers. He therefore incorporated
into his army a number of squadrons
of Polish lancers who proved effective against infantry especially when
they were scattered. The well drilled
squares of the British resisted all
efforts of Polish lancers, French
cuirassiers and light infantry to
break them.

The nineteenth century saw the
introduction of a new and tremend-
ously important firearms system.
Although there had been improvements to the basic flintlock system
during the eighteenth century there
had been no radically new ideas
since the early seventeenth. The
answer to many of the problems of
the flintlock were to be solved by
an obscure Scottish clergyman.

The flintlock was simple and

Above:
The Battle of Marengo on 14th June 1800 ended in a victory for Napoleon although at first it seemed certain that the Austrians had won. With courage and nerve Napoleon refused to recognize defeat and held his ground until reinforcements arrived.
Palais de Versailles.

Right:
Typical of many European armies is this French *Chasseur de Vincennes* of the Second Empire (1852–1871). He is armed with a 1866 Chassepot bolt action needle rifle.

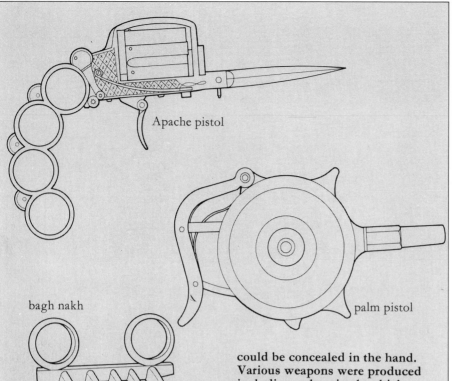

Apache pistol

bagh nakh

palm pistol

SECRET WEAPONS

When the wheellock was first developed it was possible for the first time to make small, easily concealed pistols. From the late sixteenth century onwards gunmakers have continued to produce pistols that are either very small or can be hidden in some other way. One of the earliest ideas was to combine the pistol with another weapon, and swords with a pistol fitted into the hilt were made from the seventeenth century onwards. Pistols were also fitted onto clubs, spears and even crossbows. There were a few oddities such as knives and forks with small flintlock pistols fitted into the handles. When the revolver and metal cartridge had been perfected then the possibilities were greatly increased. Another popular idea of the nineteenth century was to combine the pistol with a penknife and there are several versions of this type of weapon. Pistols were combined with other simple weapons. The best known example was the so-called Apache pistol which could serve equally well as a dagger, pistol or knuckle duster.

An alternative to combining the pistol with another weapon was to make it so small that it could be concealed in the hand. Various weapons were produced including palm pistols which were held in the hand with only the barrel protruding between the fingers. To fire it the fist was clenched and this operated the mechanism. Another popular idea was to hide the pistol in an apparently harmless purse which had a normal compartment for money whilst the other concealed a small pistol.

Beloved of the Western film producer was the small, large bore, percussion pistol designed and produced by Henry Deringer. These became so popular that they were copied by other makers who avoided patent problems by calling them Derringers. These are still made today and use ordinary cartridges.

Simpler to conceal but nonetheless lethal weapons were the so-called push knife which was held in the palm of the hand with only the blade protruding. Also very unpleasant were flick knives, knives with spring activated blades which sprang out at the touch of a button. Similar, but possibly more vicious, were the tiger-claws or *bagh nakh* of India. This had four or five claw-like blades attached to a bar and was concealed in a clenched fist until a slashing cut was delivered. Possibly less lethal was the so-called cosh or black jack which was a small, padded club. In Victorian times they were often leather covered knobs fitted to the end of a piece of cane or, occasionally, whalebone handles.

efficient, but nevertheless with priming powder there were always the problems of weather, and the danger of damp and accidental loss. For the marksman there was the annoyance of the 'hangfire'. When the trigger was pressed there was an imperceptible but nevertheless relevant pause as the mechanism was activated and the spring began to move the cock forward. The cock had to move through an angle of some 45 degrees and then the incandescent sparks had to fall into the priming; the flash had to pass through the touch hole to explode the main charge of powder. Each of these actions occupied a small, but finite, amount of time and the result was a delay known as the hangfire. Where the target was a mass of men or horses, this was relatively unimportant, but it became more so to a marksman trying to hit a moving target. There is no doubt that a skilled marksman soon learned how much allowance he had to make and he obviously aimed his weapon ahead of the moving target. Another minor annoyance for a marksman was the flash of the priming. This occurred fractionally before the shot and served as a warning to a quarry that the shot from the marksman was on its way.

The Reverend Alexander Forsyth of Belhelvie, in Aberdeenshire, was a keen hunter as well as an amateur chemist and he thought that one way to reduce the hangfire would be to speed up the rate of explosion. He sought chemicals that he might add to, or substitute for, the gunpowder to speed up the shot and among the chemicals he tried were some unstable substances known as fulminates. His experiments were not successful but he realized that there was perhaps another way of tackling the problem. Since the fulminates were so unstable a sharp knock made them explode and this provided a flash. He experimented by substituting the fulminate for the flint and steel and succeeded in igniting the charge by the flash from the exploding fulminate. Soon he had produced a device which was somewhat complex and not totally reliable, known as his 'scent bottle',

Right (*from top to bottom*):
1. Pair of officers percussion pistols by
Bushell (they are half stocked). 13 inches
(33 cm).
2. Pistol using percussion pellets or
patches and fitted with a patent pan
cover which opens automatically as the
hammer moves forward. Patented 1821.
9¼ inches (23.5 cm).
3. Four barrel flintlock, tap action pistol
which discharged two barrels with
each shot. Signed Bird & Co. London,
early 19th century. 8.62 inches (21.9
cm).
4. Device for firing a cannon or perhaps
testing percussion caps for the short
barrel is set at an angle of 45°. *c*. 1860.
5. Belgian four-barrelled percussion
pistol made in Liège. The various barrels
were selected by adjusting the nose of
the hammers. *c*. 1850. 11¾ inches
(29.8 cm).

Below (*from top to bottom*):
1. Double-barrelled snaphaunce pistol
and an unusual example of a North
African gunmaker's preference for
the snaphaunce lock. Early 19th century,
14¾ inches (37.5 cm).
2. Double-barrelled percussion pistol by
W. Jackson of London. *c*. 1840. 11
inches (27.9 cm).
3. Spanish miguelet percussion pistol
with lock signed 'Usatorre'. The whole
pistol is embellished with various
styles of decoration. Note that the
mainspring is mounted on the outside
of the lockplate. *c*. 1820. 13¾ inches
(34.9 cm).

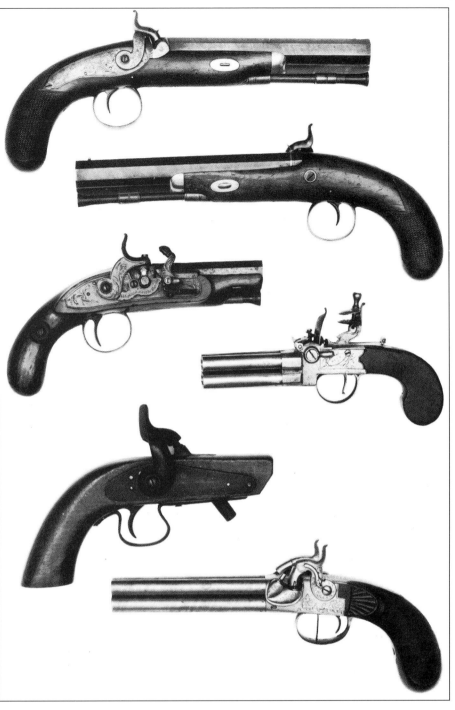

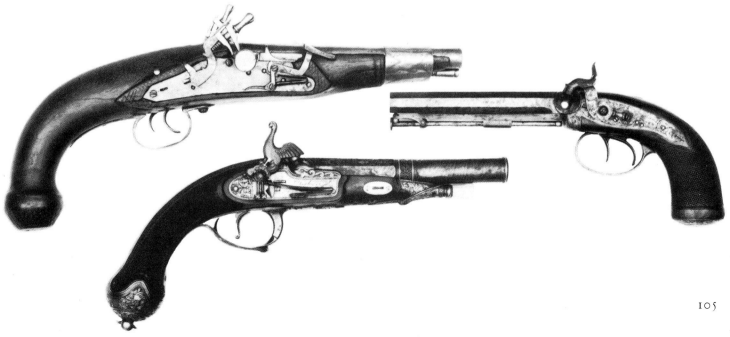

The greater firepower of industrialized armies was not always successful against less advanced weapons. During the Zulu War of 1879, the British were overwhelmed by their Zulu adversaries in the battle of Isandhlwana despite their modern breech-loading rifles.
National Army Museum, London.

Detached scent bottle lock by Forsyth. The 'bottle' is in the firing position with the spring loaded plunger being depressed by the hammer.

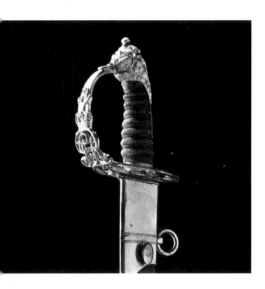

Above:
Hilt of a British flank officer's sword made of gilt. Its bugle horn emblem indicates that it belonged to an officer of a Light Company. The blade is curved. This pattern of sword was introduced in 1803.

Right:
This lithograph shows the Charge of the Heavy Brigade at the Battle of Balaclava, 1854. Less well known than the Charge of the Light Brigade which captured popular imagination, it was more successful as a military operation: the Russian cavalry were foiled in their attempts to exploit their recent capture of Turkish guns, and were routed by the British.

a name derived not from its smell but its shape. This ingenious device held a small quantity of fulminate and was attached to the side of the lock and could be rotated. When inverted it let a number of fulminate grains fall into a channel directly connected to the touch-hole. When repositioned the bottle brought a spring-loaded plunger into position above the grains of fulminate. The end of the plunger projected above the top of the scent bottle. In place of the flintlock cock there was a solid nosed hammer, but the internal mechanism was identical with the flintlock. When the trigger was pressed the hammer swung forward and hit the plunger, forcing it to detonate the grains of fulminate which exploded and flashed through the touch hole to ignite the main charge. The result was to reduce the duration of the hangfire. The fulminate also did away with the need to carry spare flints to replace worn out ones.

The idea was practical and in 1807 the Reverend Forsyth patented his system. He was encouraged to go to London to demonstrate and explain it and perhaps interest the Board of Ordnance, the body dealing with the supply of ammunition and weapons for the army and the navy. He was given facilities for research and experimentation in the Tower of London, but did not succeed in convincing the Board of Ordnance that his idea was the answer to their problems. After a brief spell he was asked to leave and the work was discontinued. His 'scent bottle' system had a number of inherent snags: having a quan-

tity of fulminate in close proximity to the exploding grains was risky for there was a danger of a chain reaction. The mechanism was also rather delicate and easily jammed. Despite these problems the possibility of a flash produced by percussion had been clearly demonstrated and other gunsmiths saw the potential of the idea and endeavoured to circumvent both Forsyth's patent and his problems. They devised simpler means of depositing the fulminate at the correct spot. They wrapped the fulminate in bits of quill, in silver foil, they stuck it on pieces of paper and they moulded it into pills – all of which were quite satisfactory but, nonetheless, rather limited solutions.

The final solution was the invention of the percussion cap which was a small, copper thimble on the inside base of which was deposited a layer of the fulminate compound. This small cap was usually made with corrugations around the side and it was fitted over a small pillar, through the centre of which a tiny hole was drilled. This pillar, the nipple, was situated over the touch hole and so connected directly to the charge. To prime the firearm it was only necessary to withdraw a copper cap from a suitable container, and place it over the nipple where the friction of the corrugations were sufficient to hold it in place. The hammer was pulled back to the full cock position and, when the trigger was pressed, fell forward and its hollow nose encircled the cap and struck it against the top of the nipple. This caused the

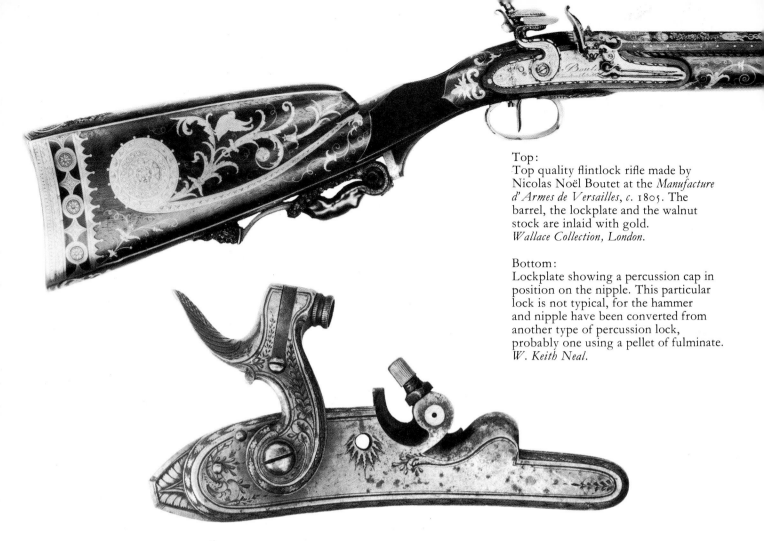

fulminate to explode and so sparked off the main charge. The cap itself split but the encircling nose of the hammer prevented it from splintering. When the gun was being reloaded the hammer was pulled back to the safe half cock position, at which point the remains of the dead cap probably fell off (if not it could easily be shaken off); the weapon was recharged, a new cap placed in position, the hammer was pulled to full cock and the weapon was ready for firing. Whose brilliant idea this percussion cap was has never been satisfactorily settled. Many people claimed to have been the inventor but on the basis of the evidence it seems likely that an American artist born in Britain, named Joshua Shaw, may have been the designer.

At first the percussion system was greeted, like all new ideas, with caution but its advantages were so apparent that soon flintlock weapons were considered to be old fashioned, obsolete and ready to be discarded. This did not necessarily mean that the whole gun was replaced since on many sporting guns the barrel was the important item and sportsmen were loath to discard a well tried and trusted weapon. Expense was another consideration and often the flintlock weapon would be converted to the new system; the frizzen, spring and priming pan were removed from the lock plate and the cock was replaced by the solid or hollow-nosed hammer. A nipple was fitted, by one means or another, into the touch-hole and the weapon was then ready for use again.

The introduction of the percussion cap opened up a whole new exciting field for the maker of firearms. The great majority of weapons so far produced had been single shot and despite all the ingenious methods tried no effective multi-shot weapon had yet been produced. The big problem with flintlock weapons was the need for repriming, and, in the case of multibarrel weapons, that of ensuring that the frizzen was correctly situated to fire each charge. With the adoption of the percussion cap and nipple, the problem was much simplified. Two common solutions were produced. The old idea of the multibarrel weapon with a metal cylinder drilled with five or six separate chambers each with a nipple at the breech end, was updated. The block was fitted into a frame with a hammer so situated that it could engage with each of the nipples in turn as the whole block was rotated either by hand or mechanically. When the bores were loaded and each nipple capped, the weapon was ready to fire five or six shots. This could be done simply by pressing the trigger the requisite number of times.

These pepperbox revolvers (the name was derived from the effect of looking at the business end of the barrel block) were very muzzle heavy and were quite inaccurate. There was also always the danger of a chain reaction, in which one exploding percussion cap would set off all the others so that instead of six single shots there was a single, six shot volley. This would be disconcerting and somewhat self-defeating! Pepperboxes appeared in the 1830s and 1840s and en-

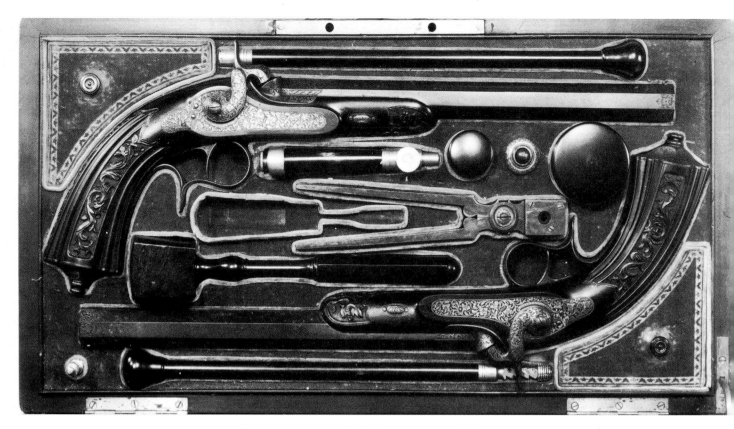

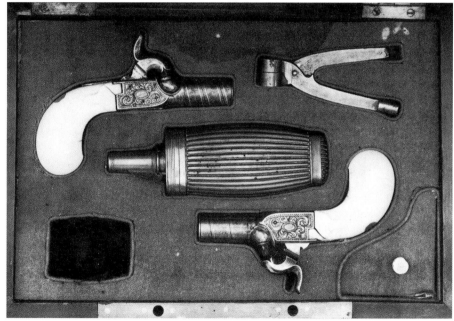

Above:
Pair of percussion duelling pistols cased with nearly all accessories, and marked 'Gauvais à Paris', *c*. 1850. The pistols are decorated in the usual French style and all the components slot into contoured spaces in the tray.

Right:
Pair of Belgian percussion pocket pistols. The barrels are rifled although with such a short barrel the effect, if any, would be very slight. The butts are ivory and the pistols have concealed triggers. They are cased with a powder flask and bullet mould. *c*. 1840. 4.12 inches (10.5 cm).

joyed a fair amount of popularity. However, in America, a much better answer was being developed by a hard-headed American business man named Samuel Colt.

Tradition has it that he worked on his idea while on a sea voyage to India; whether or not this is the case, he still produced the first really practical, mass produced, interchangeable-part revolver. This great innovation did not prove immediately successful, and his first factory even went bankrupt because there were not enough

takers for this ingenious percussion revolver. With luck, and the assistance of a Texas ranger named Colonel Walker, Colt produced a new and improved version and the design of this weapon was so good that its shape has remained virtually unchanged to the present day. In 1847 Colt produced his first big revolver. It was known as the Old Army Model or Dragoon revolver and fired a ball or conical nosed bullet .44 inches in diameter. It was heavy, weighing $4\frac{1}{2}$ pounds, but Colt had sought the advice of

well qualified arms manufacturers and produced a rifled barrel $7\frac{1}{2}$ inches long, so that the accuracy of this pistol, coupled with its rate of fire, represented a really big advance on the older, single shot weapons. Loading was comparatively simple: powder and ball were placed in each of the cylinder's chambers and the bullet was then rammed home by an ingeniously designed lever situated beneath the barrel. A cap was placed on each nipple and the weapon was ready to fire. Loose powder and ball or

Top:
The breech of an American breech-loading carbine, based on a patent taken out by J. H. Merrill in July 1858. It was loaded directly into the breech by raising the long lever which withdrew a plug giving access to the breech. It is a type known as a capping breechloader, as a cap was still required for detonation.

Centre:
Percussion pepperbox by Smith, *c*. 1840. This is a self-cocking model with the cylinder rotating and the bar hammer rising and falling by pressure on the trigger. Overall length $7\frac{3}{4}$ inches (19.7 cm), barrel $2\frac{3}{4}$ inches (7 cm), bore $\frac{1}{3}$ inch (8.5 mm).
Published by permission of Birmingham Museums and Art Gallery.

Bottom:
Pair of percussion pistols – so small that they were called muff pistols – in a small case. The box is satinwood with some gold decoration and a satirical painting of a duel. The pistols are only $3\frac{1}{4}$ inches (8.3 cm) long and have concealed triggers and safety catches. Made by J. Siddons, 1830.

Opposite:
This painting of 'Surprise Attack' by Charles Schreyvogel is interesting in that it clearly shows the U.S. troops armed with the long-barrelled, single-action Army Colt revolver. The Indian is shown with a lever action Winchester rifle although few were lucky enough to own such weapons.
Thomas Gilcrease Institute of American Art, Tulsa, Oklahoma.

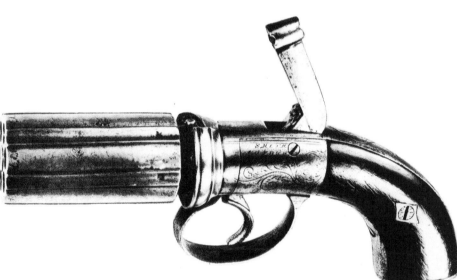

paper cartridges could be used and it was also possible, but not necessarily quicker, to have a series of loaded cylinders so that one could be removed and a new one put into place ready to fire again. Another advantage of this revolver was the interchangeability of its parts for they were mass produced and, in theory, each piece would fit any revolver of the same type.

Colt's sales began to build up and he produced a smaller version of the pistol in 1848 with a .31-inch bullet. In 1851, Colt attended the Great Exhibition in London. In the same year he had produced what has proved to be one of his most popular models: the Old Model Navy pistol which fired a small bullet, only .36 inch in diameter through a $7\frac{1}{2}$-inch barrel. It was accurate, easy to load, rugged and very reliable. When he came to England he found a market as yet untapped and with his skill at promoting his product, he began to

exploit it. So rosy did he see his prospects that he set up a factory in London which was to last for some six years. This upset the established gun trade in England who, perhaps childishly but not unnaturally, resented the appearance of this fast talking, hard headed American business man. This stimulated the production of British revolvers and a number of very famous names began to emerge in this field. The leader, and one to hold the field for some time, was Robert Adams; he was followed by Webley, Daws and Tranter, who all produced very good, solid, reliable percussion revolvers.

The main way in which Colt's revolvers differed from the early English ones was in the method of firing. The British revolvers tended to be self-cocking in that the hammer was raised, the cylinder rotated and the shot fired by pressure on the trigger. On the Colt revolvers the hammer had to be pulled back by

hand and this action turned the cylinder and cocked the mechanism; the trigger merely fired the weapon. Both systems had their advantages. Double action made for a higher rate of fire but, in the hands of an average shot, it was probably less accurate as the work done required extra power and the trigger had to be pulled quite hard. It was only a skilled hand that could keep the weapon steady whilst pressing the trigger. There was a tendency for the pistol to turn slightly – a problem still encountered today. The single action made for a slower rate of fire, but there was less pressure to activate the trigger and this would probably, all things being equal, make for more accurate shooting. There were attempts to overcome this problem and later British weapons were made so that they could be cocked either manually or by pressure on the trigger. One British maker, William Tranter, produced a double trigger

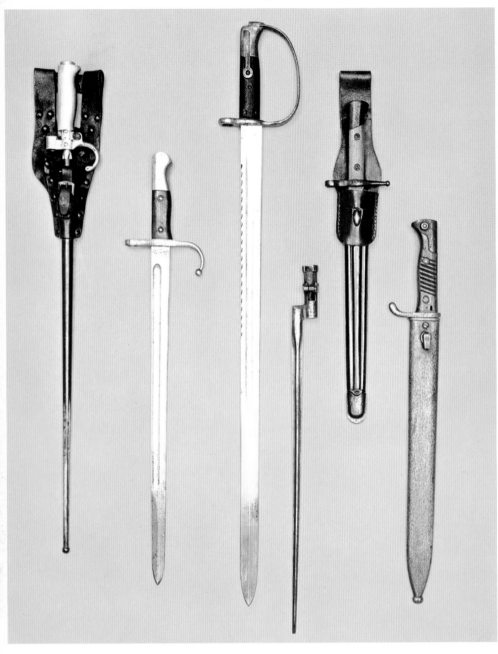

Continental bayonets. *From left to right:*
1. White metal hilt, Lebel bayonet.
French, 1886–1935.
2. Mauser bayonet with Turkish
markings. 25¾ inches (65.4 cm).
3. British Martini Henry bayonet with
saw back. 31⅛ inches (79.7 cm).
4. Russian 1891 socket bayonet. 19⅝
inches (49.8 cm).
5. Italian Carcano bayonet, 1891. 16¾
inches (42.5 cm).
6. German Mauser, 1895–1905. 19¾
inches (50.2 cm).

weapon in which the mechanism
was cocked and the cylinder rotated by pressing on the lower
trigger. A very slight pressure
on the top trigger fired the weapon.
One result of the increased supply
of revolvers was a greater use of
holsters carried on the belt, as
opposed to those fitted to the saddle.

At the same time as these changes
were taking place in the revolver,
improvements in machines were
permitting the mass production of
rifle barrels. Interest in rifles had
grown steadily from the beginning
of the century. Napoleon had not
been over impressed with rifles, but
he had had some distributed to units
in his army. The British had, with a
certain degree of reluctance, reached
the conclusion that the rifle might

have a military use, and, in 1800,
they instituted the Corps of Rifle-
men, later to become the 95th
Regiment or the Rifle Brigade, who
used the Baker flintlock rifle. This
was a fine weapon although, as
with most muzzle-loading rifles, it
was rather difficult to load. It was
essential that the bullet be very
firmly seated for the rifling had to
bite into the lead in order to turn
the bullet on its passage along the
barrel. If the bullet was tight-fitting,
it was obviously not easy to push
it down into the breech. Most of
the ordinary line infantry were
still armed with a Brown Bess
musket. The British later adopted
other rifles such as the Brunswick
in 1837 which was not a very popular weapon.

It was only during the Crimean
War (1854–56), that the desper-
ately weak supply situation of the
British Army came to light. The
government set up a big arms factory at Enfield, just outside London, to begin manufacturing the
1853 Enfield percussion rifle. This
weapon fired a bullet .577 inch in
diameter and proved an accurate
and reliable weapon.

All the rifles so far discussed –
Baker, Brunswick and Enfield –
were muzzle-loading, which meant
that their rate of fire was never very
high. The problems of loading
a rifle, which involved pushing a
bullet down the whole length of
the barrel, have already been
mentioned. The difficulty increased
as the number of rounds fired rose,
for the grooves tended to be
blocked with unburnt grains of
powder, the residue of the burnt
powder, grease and dirt. The solution to both problems was to
load in the bullet and powder at
the breech end. It was not a new
concept for some breech-loading
weapons had been produced from
the sixteenth century onwards but
these had been mostly inefficient,
expensive and dangerous. There
were one or two notable exceptions,
for example, the breech-loading,
flintlock rifle designed by Captain
Patrick Ferguson and demonstrated
by him in June 1776. Access to
the breech was gained by turning
the trigger guard which was
attached to a threaded plug. The

plug rotated and lowered to reveal the breech, powder and ball were inserted, the trigger guard was turned back and the breech was closed. The Ferguson rifle saw limited service in the American War of Independence but was then forgotten.

A simple compromise to overcome the 'tight fit' problem was devised by Claude Etienne Minie who used a bullet slightly smaller that the internal diameter of the rifled barrel. It was easy to push home but when the powder exploded the gases forced a small plug set in the base to push into the hollow bullet and expand it slightly so that it gripped the rifling.

Another more radical approach was made by the Prussians, who in 1848 adopted the Dreyse Needle gun. This rifle used a cartridge which contained the bullet, powder and a percussion cap inside the powder. To load it, a bolt was pulled back to give access to the breech and the cartridge was fitted in. The bolt was then closed sealing the breech, and a long needle was pulled back to lock under tension. When the trigger was pressed the needle flew forward, entered the breech, pierced the paper cartridge, and struck the cap so exploding the

Top:
By the late nineteenth century the only helmets still in general use were those worn by troops mainly for ceremonial purposes. This Imperial Russian helmet is surmounted by an elaborate eagle crest.
Historical Research Unit, London.

Bottom:
Painting showing the Earl of Cardigan leading the Charge of the Light Brigade during the Crimean war. Two Russian Cossacks are attacking him with their lances.
National Army Museum, London.

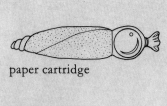

paper cartridge

Pauly cartridge

Lefaucheux pin-fire cartridge

rim-fire cartridge

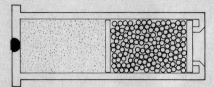

centre-pin cartridge

shotgun cartridge

rocket ball

CARTRIDGES

The first cartridges were of paper rolled round to form a tube which held a charge of powder and the lead ball. In 1835 Lefaucheux designed a cartridge with a brass head which held a percussion cap. This cap was struck by a pin which protruded from the side. This was the pin-fire cartridge. In 1860 Smith & Wesson patented the rim-fire cartridge which had the detonating compound deposited inside a rim at the base of the case. It is still used today, mostly for .22 calibre. In the mid-1860s the centre-fire, metal case cartridge was developed and had the considerable advantage that once fired the case could be reloaded.

The primer was set in the centre of the base and the hammer had a sharp nose which struck the cap.

The design of a cartridge depends on its purpose and those for rifles are normally much larger than those for revolvers and pistols. Those for most revolvers and rifles have a rim so that a little hooked arm, the extractor, can hook the empty case out of the breech after it has been fired. Cartridges for automatics do not usually have a rim for this would hinder the working of the mechanism; they have a ridge cut in the case near the base so that the extractor can still remove them.

Top right:
U.S. percussion weapons.
Top: Percussion pistol carbine, Springfield Model 1855, calibre .58. It has a Maynard primer using a tape of caps. The stock is, of course, detachable. Overall length 28¼ inches (71.75 cm).
Middle & Bottom: Different versions of the carbine made by Sharps Rifle Manufacturing Co. of Hartford, Connecticut. It was a breech loader and a very strong weapon. Some were made with a coffee grinder built into the butt.
Kenten Collection.

Bottom right:
Cutting from *Illustrated London News* of May 1868 on the French version of the Dreyse Needle Gun. It was a breech-loading weapon which used much the same firing mechanism, and was called the Chassepot rifle.

Bottom left:
Lefaucheux pin-fire shot gun. The small slots to accommodate the 'pins' are just visible at the top of the breech.
Tower of London Armouries.

Below:
The soldiers of the Queen's Own Corps of Guides (Infantry) of the Indian Army in 1897 are armed with the Martini-Henry. The rifles have the longer lever fitted to the trigger guard – a feature of the later models of this weapon.
National Army Museum, London.

charge and firing the bullet. There were still problems with this weapon but basically the idea was sound and other nations produced their own versions.

Efforts were also being made to improve the design, construction and performance of the cartridge. By the 1860s, the ideas of the French manufacturers were being developed by two British inventors, George Daw and Colonel Boxer. By 1867 the result was a cartridge with a metal base incorporating a cap and a brass case. The hammer now had to have a projecting, pointed nose which struck the percussion cap.

The new cartridge was efficient and practical, but there were still problems. Most armies held enormous numbers of percussion rifles which were now obsolete and, not unnaturally, governments were loath to undertake the cost of re-equipping their forces. England looked for a cheap system of converting her percussion weapons into breech-loaders to take the new cartridges. The experts considered some fifty different ideas and settled for one produced by Jacob Snider from New York. Some 2 inches of the barrel were removed from the breech end and a metal block, hinged on the right, was inserted in its place. A pin passed through the block and terminated just where the cap was set in the base of the cartridge. The percussion hammer hit the pin which struck the cap and fired the cartridge. The new Boxer cartridge worked well although there were problems with its extraction.

Many of these breech-loading rifles suffered, in varying degrees, from the problem of obturation, which simply means a gas escape from the breech. The various systems all tried to overcome the problem but with the metal centre-fire cartridge the trouble disappeared, opening the way for many new developments. The gunmakers were now set to produce a practical, repeating breech-loading rifle. Like so many other advances this idea had a long ancestry going back at least to the seventeenth century; the first real step, however, was made in 1848 by two Americans,

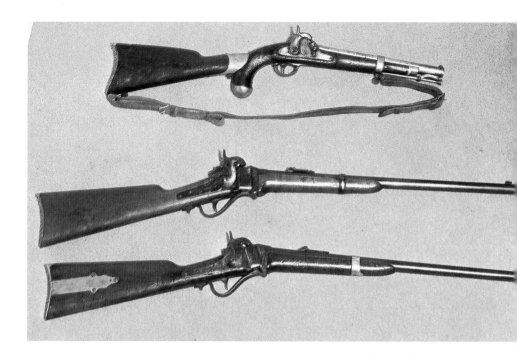

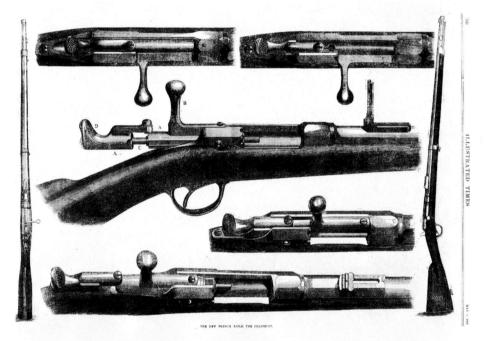

Walter Hunt and Lewis Jennings. Their repeating rifle, operated by a lever, was taken up and developed by the famous partnership of Daniel Wesson and Horace Smith and they produced the Volcanic repeating pistol and carbine. The Volcanics were not without their problems but Oliver Winchester took over the firm and, with the help of the designer Benjamin Henry, came up with a lever-operated rifle that really worked. Henry developed rim-fire cartridges in which the fulminate was spread over the whole of the inside of the base instead of being concentrated in a centrally placed cap.

Fifteen of these cartridges were housed in a tubular magazine situated beneath the barrel. When operated, the lever extracted a cartridge from the magazine, fed it into the breech and locked the breech ready for firing. In 1866 an altered Henry became the first of the famous Winchester repeating rifles.

In Britain the old Snider had served its purpose and a new weapon, designed as a breech-loader, was needed. A long series of tests were undertaken and finally, in 1871, a new single-shot rifle was adopted. It had a barrel with rifling designed by Alexander

Above:
Cutting from *Illustrated London News* of February 1891, on the new Lee-Metford magazine, bolt-action rifle, officially introduced to the British Army in 1889.

Below:
Mauser automatic pistol with its wooden holster which also serves as a shoulder stock. This is one of the earlier models, for it has a 'cone hammer'.
National Army Museum, London.

Henry of Edinburgh and an action patented by a Swiss, Frederick von Martini. This weapon had a breech opened by pulling down a long extension to the trigger guard. It fired a .45 cartridge and was a reasonably satisfactory weapon although, being only single shot, it was rather old fashioned.

By 1871 the Germans had Mauser rifles with an eight-round magazine and Britain felt it was time the army had a magazine rifle also. In 1888 a Lee Metford rifle with a calibre of .303 inches was adopted. It was a bolt-operated rifle with a magazine holding eight rounds. In 1892 a new cartridge was introduced and this was loaded with the new smokeless explosive. One of the problems with all firearms in bulk had been the massive amount of smoke generated by hundreds of cartridges, but thanks to a French chemist, Paul Vieille, a new type of powder which produced virtually no smoke was developed in the 1880s.

Similar important changes had taken place in the design of revolvers. Colt had dominated this field until 1857 when Smith and Wesson put a breech-loading revolver on the market which used a metal cartridge. They held a master patent for a system of loading the cylinder from the rear which had been designed by Rollin White. Until 1869 no other maker could use this idea for Smith and Wesson alone had the right to do so. When their monopoly ended nearly every gunsmith tried his hand at designing new, breech-loading revolvers, but the outstanding one was Colt's Single Action Army revolver first put on the market in 1873. Its cylinder held six shots and the empty cases were ejected by means of a spring-loaded rod set below and to one side of the barrel. The success of its design is clearly emphasized by the fact that it has been in virtually continuous production ever since.

Although there had been tremendous developments in firearms other weapons had changed little. Most military rifles still had bayonets although the style of attaching them was more varied: a lug on the barrel and a spring

Smith and Wesson cartridge revolver of 1881. To load or eject a spring catch situated just above the hammer was operated so that the barrel and cylinder could be swung down. The barrel is 6½ inches (16.6 cm) and the revolver was chambered for .44 Smith & Wesson Russian cartridges. *Winchester Gun Museum, New Haven, Connecticut.*

catch on the hilt of the bayonet was common but socket bayonets had by no means disappeared. A great variety of styles were produced but this basically was the only edged weapon still used in war. The officers' sword was now mainly ceremonial but cavalry still made some use of this weapon. Many army authorities, however, were beginning to realize that the new firearms meant that the cavalry were becoming outmoded.

The only new edged weapon to to develop in the nineteenth century was the Bowie knife. Today the name is used for a whole range of daggers and knives, but the original knife designed by Bowie was large-bladed and had a marked curve on one side of the edge and a cusped cut on the back which was sharpened to give a false edge. Its weight enabled it to be used for chopping, the point for stabbing and the long blade for cutting. The undoubted practical value of the bowie knife, together with the glamorous end of its maker who was killed fighting for Texas in the Battle of the Alamo in 1836, ensured that it found a ready market. Ironically, this essentially American edged weapon was produced in bulk in Britain.

Armour had, like edged weapons, disappeared from the battlefield although there was apparently still a sale for body armour among the

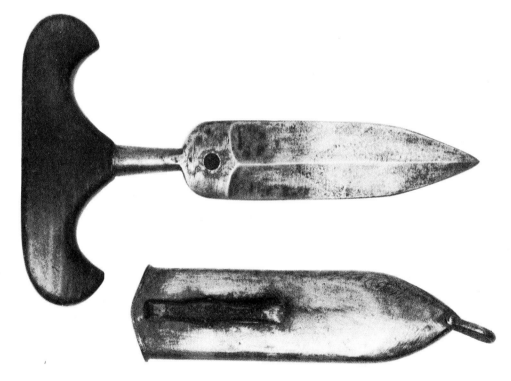

troops. During the American Civil War (1861–65) many firms offered private armour for sale but it was no longer a government issue. The American Civil War has been described as the first of all modern wars – a title well justified on many counts. It saw the introduction of many modern aids such as armoured ships, telegraph and photography, and in particular of repeating, breech-loading firearms. In this it set the pattern for nearly all future wars.

Push dagger which was held with the bar in the palm of the hand and the blade projecting between the knuckles. The dagger was used to deliver a blow by a punch or push in the manner of an Indian *katar*.

The Twentieth Century

By the end of the nineteenth century, the weapons of the modern age had developed. The only change was to be in matters of detail. By the late 1890s almost every army in the world was equipped with a magazine repeating rifle of some form or other. Each nation had carried out its own tests and chose, for a variety of reasons, differing models, each manufactured by a well-known maker. Mannlicher, or variations, were chosen by Italy, Holland, Austria-Hungary, Roumania and Greece; Mauser by Turkey, Portugal, Spain and Germany; Lebel by France and Ross by Canada. They were virtually all manually operated, bolt-action weapons. A mechanical locking device had to be operated by hand in order to extract the empty case, take out a round from the magazine, feed it into the breech and cock the mechanism before the trigger was pressed. Each of these rifles was fitted with its own particular kind of bayonet which were generally long with blades of around 16 to 18 inches in length. The majority of them were now fitted to the muzzle by means of the lug and spring catch.

The twentieth century, like the nineteenth, opened with war. In Africa the Boers, descendants of the Dutch settlers, were fighting the British; the Americans were engaged in the Philippines; Russia and Japan were at war between 1904 and 1905. These were the first large-scale wars in which auto-

matic weapons had been used, and the military world watched with interest to see how the new weapons would affect the outcome. One factor in the effectiveness of troops is their ability to maintain a high rate of missle discharge. The archer was reckoned to be good if he could loose twelve arrows a minute; a musketeer could reckon on two shots a minute. By the 1890s a British soldier could attain some fifteen shots a minute with his Martini-Henry and this figure was greatly improved when the Lee-Enfield magazine rifle came into service. However, even these bolt-

Above:
Luger automatic pistols. The top one is the rare 1900 carbine type with hand grip and butt stock. The lower is artillery with an 8-inch long barrel with holster and snail drum. Both fire a 9-mm bullet.
Pattern Room, Royal Small Arms Factory, Enfield.

Opposite:
This painting from the First World War has British and Australian troops advancing into a captured village. It is presumably earlier than 1915 as none have steel helmets. They carry SMLE rifles and the officer has a Webley revolver.

action rifles were hand operated and magazines had to be recharged, since most had a capacity of only ten rounds. Although the rate of fire had increased enormously it was still limited to the speed of the operator.

What the arms makers sought to do was to eliminate the human factor in recharging the weapon, and increase firepower by making the whole thing automatic. They wanted to construct a weapon that would automatically eject an empty cartridge case, feed in a new one and fire itself, repeating this sequence for as long as required. The idea was not new and the nineteenth century had known some very efficient repeating weapons. The American Civil War had seen the Gatling gun, invented by Dr. Richard Gatling in 1862, in action. This was a hand operated weapon which had a group of barrels arranged in a circle. As the handle was turned the barrels rotated and as they turned they were fed with cartridges; as the cartridges were fired the empty cases were ejected and a new one inserted. Cartridges were fed in from a box or hopper situated above the gun. The gun had not been very effective with the early cartridges but when metal cased ones were introduced the Gatling gun had proved its worth time and

FORBIDDEN WEAPONS

During the nineteenth century, an agreement was made that weapons should not needlessly aggravate suffering. As early as 1868, nations were formulating rules as to which weapons could or could not be used. Missiles which were barbed or which were coated with poison were excluded, so too were 'irregularly shaped' bullets: the most infamous of all such projectiles was the so-called dum-dum bullet, which was apparently first manufactured at the British arsenal of that name in India. This lead bullet had a deep cross cut into the nose so that the projectile would spread on impact and cause a more severe wound. A very similar effect is produced by some modern, hollow-nosed bullets. These have a metal coating which stops just short of the nose and the lead bullet so exposed has a deep recess in it so that it will also flatten on impact. A similar effect is produced by high velocity bullets.

Poison gas, first used on a large scale by the Germans in the First World War, was also forbidden in 1925, as was germ or bacteriological warfare. This prohibition was not ratified by the U.S.A. or Japan but fortunately neither form of weapon was used in the Second World War. Whether the same restriction could also be applied to tear and C.S. gas has been keenly debated.

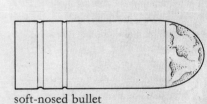

soft-nosed bullet

tubed bullet

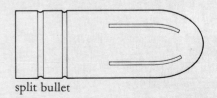

split bullet

These dainty .22 revolvers were popular with women for self defence, hence their name Ladysmiths.
Top: 3rd model Ladysmith, 1911–1921. Nickel plated and shown with its suede purse. 3½-inch barrel (8.9 cm).
Bottom: 1st Model Ladysmith, 1902–1906. 3-inch barrel (7.62 cm).

time again. Many nations adopted it including the British, and it saw action in many parts of the world. In theory it could attain a rate of fire of 600 rounds per minute (r.p.m.) but in practice between 250 and 300 seems to have been normal.

Between the years 1860 and 1880 a number of manually operated machine-guns were produced and used with varying degrees of success. The French miscalculated on the efficiency and effectiveness of their multibarrel *mitrailleuse* and instead of victory against the Prussians it brought only disappointment and defeat. Britain set up a Machine-Gun Committee in 1880, and various models were examined and tested including the Nordenfelt which could fire 1000 r.p.m. They also had designs for a machine gun with a single barrel and a rate of fire of 180 r.p.m.

The man who did most to develop the new automatic weapon was Sir Hiram Maxim, born in America in 1840. Originally he was nothing to do with the gun trade for he had been an electrician and a manager of an electricity factory. He turned his mind to the problem of automatic weapons when someone suggested to him that he was wasting his time inventing useful things and if he could produce a means of killing more people, more

quickly, he would make a fortune. He came to England and set himself up in Hatton Garden at the centre of the jewellery trade.

He saw and appreciated a fact known to almost everybody: that for every action there is an equal and opposite reaction. As the cartridge fired and pushed the bullet forward there was an opposite reaction, which tried to push back the case. Maxim saw that this recoil could probably be used to power the mechanism. He arranged for it to stretch a spring which then compressed and pulled everything back to where it had been before the shot was fired. He worked on the problem and came up with a theoretical solution, produced a prototype which, through a combination of genius and luck, worked first go. He had produced the first truly automatic weapon and as long as ammunition was fed in his gun would continue firing. His ammunition feed consisted of a long canvas belt with the cartridges pushed through a series of loops. Once the mechanism was cocked and the trigger was pressed it would continue firing for just as long as there was ammunition or until some mechanical fault or jamming occurred.

Maxim soon managed to interest the British army and before long his gun was sought after by nations

throughout the world. It had a rate of fire of up to 600 r.p.m. which could be reduced, quite simply, to as few as 2 r.p.m. Maxim's weapon was fairly simple and basically sound and was adopted by a whole range of nations. He co-operated with the famous British armaments firm of Vickers and the outcome was the Vickers-Maxim machine-gun which became the heavy machine-gun of the British army for many many years.

Once the principle had been demonstrated, there was a flood of other designs that performed the same function. They varied in detail but most worked on two main principles. Whichever principle was followed, the object was to use some of the spare energy produced when the charge exploded. Some, like Maxim's gun operated on the recoil principle so that as the bullet left the case was kicked back and this energy was used to operate the mechanism. Others utilized some of the gas produced by the explosion. A small hole was drilled into the side of the barrel, and as the bullet was driven up the barrel some of the gas was syphoned off through this tube and fed back to where its power was used to operate the mechanism.

Most European armies acquired various models and the demand for machine-guns increased. France had the Hotchkiss and the Chauchat and Germany had the Maxim. There was no doubt of the machine-gun's efficiency for already it had seen action in India and Africa, and had proved devastating in its power to pour out bullets at a rate which was previously undreamed of.

The coming of the machine-gun was to prove the finishing blow for the old chivalry of Europe. For centuries the mounted knight had dominated the battlefields and had been more or less immune from all weapons. The longbow had altered matters in favour of the infantry but there was still a feeling that the cavalry had a very important part to play. Gunpowder reduced their importance even more but no military man could believe that there was no longer a place for them in the forces. Every army still had a large number of mounted units.

Breech-loading rifles really made the horse obsolete in warfare but until the Boer War the machine-gun had not seen service on a large scale and no one was sure what its effect would be. In 1893 and 1894, the machine-gun had been used against the Matabele in the Transvaal and had held off their attacks with ease. In the Sudan at the Battle of Omdurman, it was estimated that three-quarters of the enemy casualties were caused by the British machine-gun. The First World War settled any lingering doubts about the cavalry's role in battle and for most of the four years' conflict they were forced to play a very minor and static part. From the 1920s onwards every army gradually replaced its horses with noisy, oily heavily armoured cars and tanks, often less versatile than a horse but always less vulnerable to the modern, high-powered bullet.

19th- and 20th-century sporting rifles. *From top to bottom:*
1. Belgium sporting Mauser, bolt action rifle with pistol grip and half stock.
2. Czech sporting Mauser rifle fitted with hair trigger to ensure that only minimum pressure is required to fire it.
3. .44 Colt New Lightning repeating rifle. It is loaded by operating the grip beneath the barrel.
4. Belgium 16-bore sporting gun with 5 chambered cylinder. It is a design patented by L. Ghaye and operates by moving the lever in front of the trigger guard.
5. .44 Sporting rifle by F. Barnes & Co. of London with 6-chambered cylinder.
6. .44 1866 Winchester rifle, and one of the first popular repeating rifles.

The Vickers-Maxims were normally mounted on a tripod which made them heavy and slow to move and the designers began to think about a lighter, more versatile machine-gun. One of the most effective of these was designed by Isaac Lewis in 1911 and it operated with a coiled spring for motive power and was operated by gas that had been syphoned off. In June 1912 a Lewis gun was taken into the air in one of the Wright brother's aircraft by a Captain Chandler, who successfully fired at a large target placed on the ground. Contrary to expressed fears, the aircraft did not shake to pieces or crash and aerial warfare had made a hesitant start.

The Lewis gun was chosen for this experiment because it was cooled by air and not, like the Maxim, by water: this helped to reduce the weight even further. One of the problems with all automatic weapons is the very considerable amount of heat generated by the explosion and the passage of the bullet along the barrel. There is the risk of a round 'cooking off', in other words being fired by the heat in the breech, and also seizing up due to expansion of the metal. Every automatic weapon has to make provision for the removal of this heat. Heavy machine-guns have in the past used water but today most use a flow of air to cool the barrel.

Top:
Thompson submachine-guns.
Above: Model 1928 A1. *Below:* Model M1. Both weapons fire the .45 ACP cartridge which could be loaded into magazines of 20, 30, 50 or 100 round capacity. The top model has a Cutts compensator fitted at the muzzle designed to prevent the muzzle rising when the gun was fired.
Royal Small Arms Factory, Enfield.

Above:
A Ross rifle, .303 Mk. III, made in Canada by the Ross Rifle company. It has an oval, silver plaque in the butt indicating that it was presented to Winston Churchill in 1914 by the Canadian Minister of Militia and Defence, S. Hughes.

The Lewis gun was quite light but it was still not really suitable for firing unsupported and the next step was to design a gun that could be fired without a stand. John Browning, a master designer in the world of firearms, had produced some very fine hand and shoulder guns and in 1890 he had designed a machine-gun for Colts Manufacturing Company which was quickly adopted by the U.S. Navy. Browning began work on an automatic rifle which could be supported by a sling across the shoulder and fired either single shot or fully automatic. In February 1917 he demonstrated the Browning Automatic Rifle (B.A.R.) and its rate of fire was 400 r.p.m. although the magazine capacity was only thirty shots. The B.A.R. was good and was consequently adopted by the United States, but it was still just a little cumbersome and, as always in the history of gun-manufacture, other designers followed Browning's lead.

One step in this direction was to use a smaller cartridge so reducing weight and size and the Villar Perosa light machine-gun used a pistol cartridge, in this case a 9-mm Parabellum. Although still a little primitive, the Villar Perosa worked, and it was soon improved on. Beretta, the Italian gunmaker, produced a far more efficiently designed model and in 1918 the submachine-gun was created. In 1921 the best known of all submachine-guns was put onto the arms market: this was the Thompson or Tommy gun. This weapon used a .45 round which was inserted in a spring operated, circular drum magazine with a capacity of 50 or 100 r.p.m. It was designed to offer single shot or automatic fire at a rate of 800 r.p.m. It somehow caught the public imagination and its name became almost synonymous with the submachine-gun although it was only one of many. In Germany the Schmeisser was in production from 1918 and was to be developed

Although rapidly becoming obsolete the cavalry lingered on in most armies until the 1920s and 30s. These two lancers are part of a patrol in Tergnier captured by the Germans in March 1918.
Imperial War Museum, London.

Above:
A painting by Ivor Hele showing Australians overrunning a German position in North Africa during the Second World War. In action can be seen Tommy guns, a Luger and Short Magazine Lee Enfield Rifles.
The Australian War Museum, Canberra.

Below:
This Mark V Sten has been stripped to show the very small number of simple components which made up this effective submachine-gun. Other versions were simpler, lacking the front pistol grip and substituting a metal stock. The magazine held 32 rounds of 9 mm cartridges.
Imperial War Museum, London.

and supplied to the German forces during the Second World War. It introduced the folding stock which is a feature of many modern weapons and is useful when space is a problem for it shortens the weapon.

During the Second World War there were considerable problems of supply and despite great efforts the armament industries could not keep up with the demand. This situation called for a re-appraisal and in Britain one solution offered was to design and produce a weapon which was simple and required only a minimum of moving parts. After many experiments the weapon produced was the Sten submachine-gun which fired a 9 mm cartridge. It looked very cheap and nasty and earned such nicknames as 'drain-pipe gun' and 'Woolworth gun' but it was cheap to produce – around £5 in 1941. Its very cheapness was a virtue for this meant that it could be dropped in quantities to the various underground and resistance units throughout Europe. The mechanism operated on the blowback principle in that the explosion drove the bullet forward and the

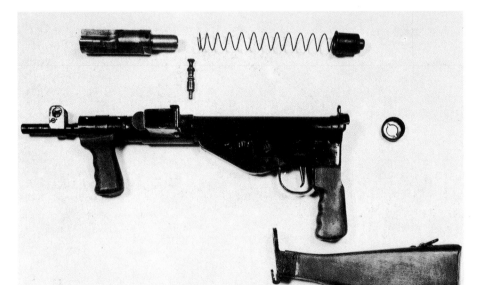

Right:
Still being made 104 years after its
introduction, the Colt single action army
revolver is today a popular handgun.
This example, in a modern holster and
belt, is a .375 magnum version.

breech-block backwards, the
breech-block being returned by a
coiled spring. Maintenance was
minimal and virtually only the
breech-block moved so oiling was
unnecessary. The magazine was
straight and fitted in from the left.
It held 32 rounds. The Sten –
named from the initials of the
designers Shepherd and Turpin
and the place Enfield – was produced in six versions although the
Mark II was probably the most
common. Its most serious weakness
was probably a rather unsafe 'safe'
position, for the cocking handle
could easily be dislodged with
disastrous results.

The nearest United States equivalent to the Sten was probably the
.45-inch M.3 submachine-gun,
sometimes described as the 'grease
gun'. Unlike the Sten it offered
only automatic fire – at a rate of
450 r.p.m.

Research has continued in this
field and weapons like the U.S.
AR15, the Israeli UZI, the Czech
Scorpion and the Russian AK47
and AKM now dominate the automatic weapons field. Experiments
continue and there is a general
trend towards smaller cartridges –
the latest British model fires a
4.85-mm bullet. The modern firearms industry, aided by developments in optics, is producing
weapons that really leave little to
the skill of the firer. The U.S. 180
rifle system uses an American 180
M2 rifle which takes a drum magazine holding 177 rounds of .22
cartridges which can be fired, single
or automatic, at a rate of 1200 r.p.m.
Coupled with the Laser Lok sight
it is a weapon to be feared. The
laser, mounted below the barrel,
projects a beam of red light so
concentrated that it has a diameter
of only three inches at 200 yards,
and to hit the mark the dot of light
is simply directed at the target;
when aligned the trigger is pressed
and a hit is certain! Failing this
the laser produces a non-perma-
nent but totally disabling blindness

Centre:
This is one of the very efficient German
machine-guns produced during the
Second World War. It is the MKb 42(H)
made by Haenel and operated on the
feedback of some of the gas generated
during the explosion of the 7.62 mm
cartridge. The magazine held 30 rounds.
*Pattern Room, Royal Small Arms Factory,
Enfield.*

Bottom:
Modern armies are being equipped more
and more with automatic weapons and
this is an experimental British model,
the EM2. It has several unusual features
such as the magazine situated behind
the trigger, the simple shoulder stock
and the forward hand grip. It fires a
4.82 mm bullet of quite a small calibre.
Royal Small Arms Factory, Enfield.

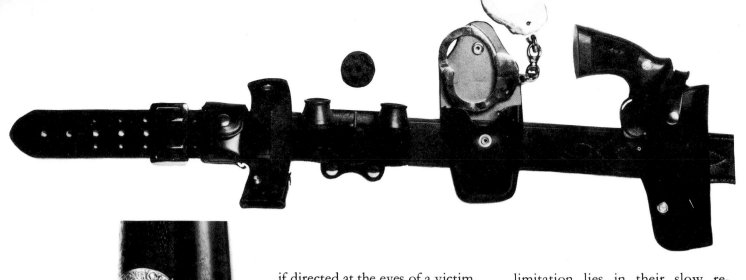

if directed at the eyes of a victim.

Submachine-guns, machine-guns, assault rifles and general purpose machine-guns all have their place in the modern armoury but there is also a demand for a repeating handgun. The revolver was well established by the 1870s with Colt's Single Action Army Model, Smith and Wessons and others, capable of accurate, reliable shooting. In 1870 Smith and Wesson produced a system of automatic ejection for the empty cases and this idea was incorporated into many other models. Swing out cylinders with a manual ejector system were soon available and the range of revolvers being made for the target shooter and hunter was very great indeed.

Developments in the design of revolvers has been restricted mainly to the use of new materials – stainless steel is very commonly used today. A great variety of calibres is available for the revolver although most use .22, .38 Special, .44 or .45. In 1902 the popular .38 Special cartridge was introduced by Smith and Wesson; this was followed by a more powerful version, the .357 Magnum cartridge in 1935 which gave nearly twice the velocity of and much greater penetrative power than the 38 Special cartridge. In 1955 they produced a .44 magnum cartridge which is powerful enough for hunting big game, and can easily penetrate a car body and engine. It is not an easy cartridge to shoot for the recoil is considerable!

Revolvers have much to recommend them as far as reliability is concerned and many whose lives may depend on a firearm prefer them for this reason. Their biggest limitation lies in their slow reloading, for the empty cases have to be ejected and then five or six new cartridges inserted into the chambers. Devices called speed loaders can be used and these will drop all the cartridges in together with one movement but even so they take time. For rapid firing the self-cocking action is essential and this means a strong pull on the trigger to activate the mechanism which, as pointed out above, increases the chances of moving the weapon off the correct aiming point.

Designers of firearms began to to think of self-loading weapons which could automatically reload and cock the weapon. The problem was to fit such a mechanism to a small hand-gun – it was easy with a machine-gun where there was plenty of room. In 1892 an Austrian designer named Anton Schonberger developed an 8-mm, self-loading weapon which was ingenious and worked on a movement of only 3/16 inch. The first really practical weapon was designed by Hugo Borchardt, a naturalized American. It was long – 14 inches – and had a rather bulky rear section with the butt set more or less at the centre of the weapon. The recoil operated a toggle arm powered by a coiled spring which pushed the cartridges in and out of the breech. The rounds were loaded into the pistol by means of a metal box which could be filled and then inserted into the butt. If several magazines were available then reloading was simple and involved only extracting the empty one and inserting a full magazine. The Borchardt and all self-loading or so-called automatic pistols are single shot weapons.

Top:
Typical police 'rig' as used by many U.S. police forces. The black leather belt is fitted with a holster with a Smith and Wesson .357 magnum revolver, handcuff and cased set of three speed loaders and two 'dumpers' which hold six rounds each.

Above:
British shotguns have always had the reputation for being the best in the world. This breech shows the quality of engraving to be found on examples of the finest by Holland and Holland, a well known, long established firm of London gunmakers.

Borchardt's pistol was rather awkward but it was basically sound. The design was improved by George Luger and in 1900 he was granted a patent for a better toggle. The Luger 9-mm Parabellum is one of the best known pistols in the world and has a certain mystique about it. Various models with barrel lengths from 4 inches to 10 inches were produced, and it was used by many armies for many years. It was the official German side arm until it was replaced in 1938 by the Walther P.38.

Another automatic which is instantly recognized is the Mauser, first put on the market in 1896. The magazine, situated in front of the trigger, and the rather straight, spindly butt are features of the weapon. It was an accurate, hard hitting weapon although it had a trick of giving a nasty gash to the unwary shooter who had gripped the butt too close to the top for the breech block slammed back rather hard and low. Most Mauser 'broom-handles' were chambered for 7.63-mm cartridges, but some took a 9-mm cartridge; these are marked with a red 9 on the butt to distinguish them since they are externally the same in appearance.

Scottish broadsword with basket hilt fitted. The bar was used to unscrew the pommel so that the basket could be removed and the simple cross-bar fitted. The two sheaths are for dress (steel) and for service (leather covered). The sword belonged to a Lieutenant in the Third Dundee Highland Volunteer Battalion, Black Watch, c. 1905.
R. Boorman.

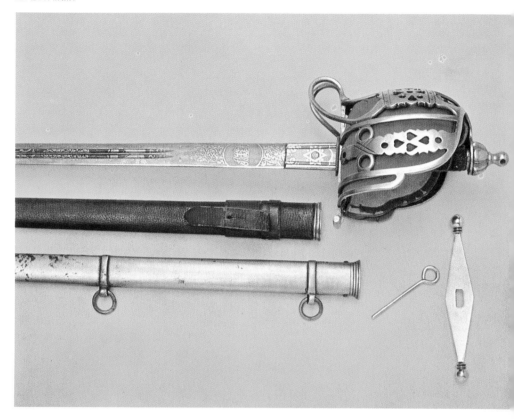

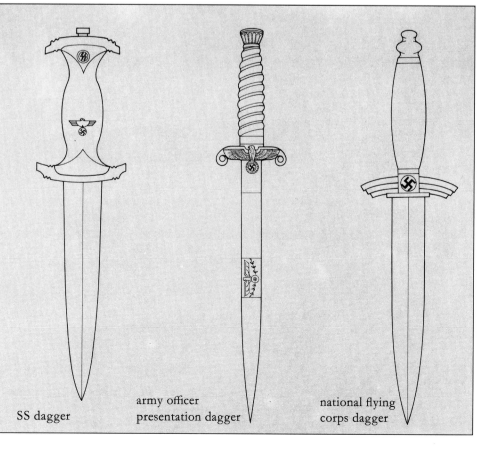

NAZI DAGGERS
When the Third Reich was formed in 1933, the sword makers of Solingen, who were hard hit by unemployment, presented Hitler with a letter opener. They also suggested that the city would benefit if a dagger became part of the uniform of Nazi Germany. The suggestion was well received and a whole range of patterns was approved. The first was for the S.A. (Sturm Abteilung) and was based on a Swiss dagger of the sixteenth century designed by Holbein. Next came a dagger for the S.S. (Schutz Staffel) which was similar but had a black grip. Various other patterns were produced for the army, navy and airforce as well as groups such as the Hitler Youth Movement, Railway Protection Force and the Fire Department.

SS dagger

army officer presentation dagger

national flying corps dagger

John Browning in the U.S.A. was largely responsible for another famous automatic, the Colt .45 which was originally designed for .38 cartridges. In official tests in 1907 a .45 Colt automatic was adopted by the U.S.A. but it did not live up to its promise and received very unfavourable reports from troops. Further work was carried out and in 1911 a new, improved model was accepted: this was a marvellous weapon. Modified in 1920, it was designated the 1911A1 and has proved itself one of the best combat pistols in the world. During the Second World War, a mass produced pistol – the Liberator – was designed to fire the Colt .45 cartridge. It was single shot and at best could only be described as crude, but for underground and resistance groups it was very welcome.

Since the 1900s a multitude of automatics have been produced in all calibres from 3-mm to .45 and with a magazine capacity of up to thirteen or more rounds. Most have to be cocked before the first shot, which involves pulling the moveable section, the slide, back round the barrel; now however some can be cocked by pressure on the trigger like a revolver.

Shotguns have undergone many changes this century and the Winchester Company introduced a repeating model as early as 1887. A pump action version was available in 1893 and today this type of shot-

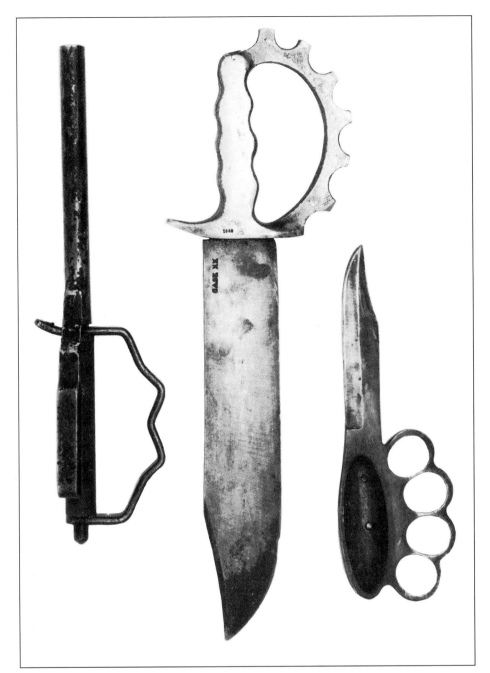

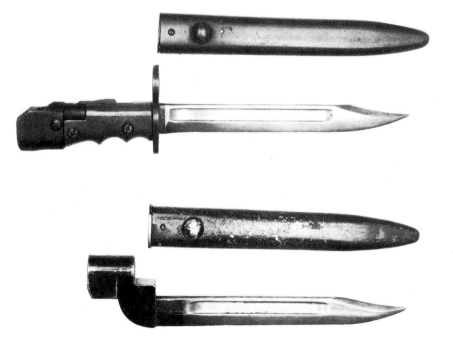

Above:
Fighting knives of the 20th century.
Left: Thin bladed knife with all-metal scabbard. First World War.
Centre: Special knife of the 1st Ranger Battalion (U.S.) with cast brass hilt incorporating a knuckle duster. Second World War.
Right: Well-made fighting knife with wooden grip and knife and knuckle duster fashioned in one. Second World War.

Left:
British bayonets and scabbards.
Above: Bowie bladed Mk. 7 which fitted the No. 4 rifle as well as the Sten gun. The top section of the grip pivots to fit the barrel.
Below: Mk. 9 socket bayonet with metal scabbard, made in 1949 for the Mk. 4 rifle. 8 inches (20.3 cm).

Left:
A variety of speed loaders, which are devices to reduce the time required to load cartridges into a revolver cylinder. The leather pouches each hold six rounds and when opened tip down to allow cartridges to fall into the hand. All the other devices operate on the basis of dropping all six cartridges directly into the cylinder.

Below:
Members of the French unit of the United Nation Forces fighting during the Korean War of 1950–53. They are operating an M.20 recoil-less rifle. First developed at the end of the Second World War, this was designed as a close support infantry weapon.

gun is one of the favoured weapons for police work. For riot control or close combat work it is extremely effective and seldom gives the 'target' a second chance to retaliate. A less lethal weapon for police work is the rubber bullet which is discharged from a large bore shoulder weapon. Various unpleasant gas projectiles such as C.N., C.S. and H.C. smoke can also be fired from the same weapon.

Vastly improved firearms had, by the beginning of this century, relegated most edged weapons to the parade-ground or the museum. Bayonets of various sizes and shapes were retained although after the First World War their use was primarily for opening tins, digging, hanging clothes and similar useful jobs. Most were made as separate weapons but some were permanently attached to the barrel. Some of these were operated by springs and when released swung forward and locked into position – an interesting return to an idea first patented in the 1790s.

Trench warfare of the First World War was a sordid, nasty business, involving hand to hand fighting,

and it brought about a revival of the dagger as a weapon of war. Frequent raids were carried out by both sides which were secret, silent operations with firearms kept only as a final resort: knuckle dusters, clubs, and daggers were the main weapons. Many troops fashioned their own from cut-down bayonets, barbed wire woven around a wooden handle and similar unpleasant devices, but soon official weapons were being developed and issued. In 1917 a trench knife which had a long, thin blade and a knuckle bow with conical projections designed as a knuckle duster was issued to U.S. troops. In 1918 a new model the Mark I trench knife was ordered and this had a much broader blade and a cast bronze knuckle duster grip. Interest lessened after 1918 but was revived in the Second World War and an American M.3 version was adopted in 1943 which was later modified to serve as a bayonet as well. In Britain a much slimmer type was adopted and was known as the Sykes-Fairburn knife which had a ridged metal grip and a tapered, double-edged blade.

Another relic of earlier times which made a considerable comeback during the First World War was body armour. By the beginning of the nineteenth century armour had virtually disappeared from the battlefields of the world. Some French cavalry at Waterloo had worn cuirasses, but this was really the last use of this bit of equipment by large numbers of troops on the battlefield. During the American Civil War there were reports of body armour being produced for sale to the troops. The First World War was the first modern war in which the idea of personal protection was revived; like the reintroduction of helmets, this reversion was largely due to trench warfare. By 1915 it was realized that a higher than expected proportion of head wounds were being numbered among the casualties. The reason for this was obvious: so many were in the trenches below ground level that falling debris, shell splinters and spent bullets dropped onto the head and shoulders. It was obvious that some form of protection should be given to the head. The French were the

first to produce a metal head-guard which was known as an Adrian after the French general who introduced it. Tradition has it that he drew his inspiration from seeing French troops using their regulation issue metal billy-cans, which were combined drinking and eating vessels, to cover their heads.

The French helmet was light with only a narrow brim and a central comb running across the skull. Both the Allies and the Germans began to experiment with these steel helmets. The British one was reminiscent of the old kettle hat with a domed skull and a narrow, slightly down-sloping brim. Inside there were pads of felt to absorb the shock and later models had far more complicated liners to fit any head and to prevent construction. In 1917 the Americans entered the First World War and adopted the British pattern steel helmet which was found to have twice the ballistic strength of the French pattern. Apart from some changes in the liner in 1936, this M.1917 helmet remained the official American pattern until June 1941, when the M.1. pattern was

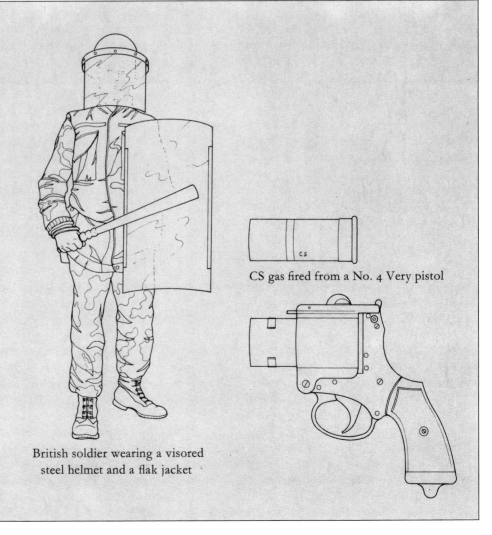

Left:
This painting showing a French assault by dawn gives some idea of the terrible conditions on the Western Front with mud and barbed wire slowing down any attack. The soldiers wear their horizon blue uniform, steel Adrian helmets and are armed with Lebel rifles.
Musée de l' Armée, Paris.

Right:
Daggers of the 3rd Reich. Two bear original Eickhorn tags.
Left to Right:
1. Dress dagger of Technical Emergency Corps: officers' model.
2. Dress dagger of Technical Emergency Corps: men's model.
3. 1st Model Air Raid Wardens' dagger: officers' model.
Colin Nunn.

RIOT GEAR

The growth of organized urban violence has led to the development of specialized deterrent weapons, essentially disabling rather than lethal. There are special guns which fire 'baton rounds', which are large diameter rubber bullets intended to stun or bruise. There are also a number of irritant gases available which can be discharged from an aerosol type spray, fired from a gun or thrown as a grenade. Most are intended to produce choking sensations, nausea and tears whilst some experimental ones are more drastic producing unconsciousness.

Protection for the forces dealing with such violence has also been developed. Steel or plastic helmets fitted with shatter-proof, transparent visors are common. Large shields to serve both for protection and crowd control are standard equipment for many police forces. Against the sniper there are several forms of so-called flak jackets which are essentially bullet proof vests. The garment is fitted with metal, plastic or ceramic materials which are extremely effective in withstanding almost all handguns and some rifle bullets.

British soldier wearing a visored steel helmet and a flak jacket

CS gas fired from a No. 4 Very pistol

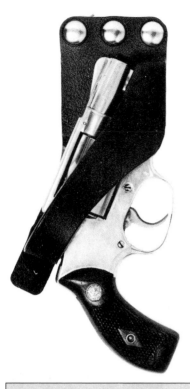 

Left:
Modern holsters designed for combat shooting. On the left is an all rubber, skeletal form and on the right a more conventional leather style. Both are for revolvers with 2-inch (5-cm) barrels.

Bottom right:
This is one of the many types of infrared sights in service throughout the world and here is fitted to the British General Purpose machine-gun. A beam of invisible infra-red radiation is projected by the top 'lamp' and the reflected rays are detected by the 'telescope' sight permitting accurate shooting in the dark up to about 480 feet.

TERRORIST WARFARE

Over the last few decades there has been a marked increase in guerilla and urban warfare by small groups seeking to gain some political end. This is not a new phenomenon, but what is new is the more sophisticated equipment at the disposal of the revolutionaries or terrorists. High powered rifles, automatic rifles, grenades, pistols and rocket launchers have all been used by different groups, many of which obtain their supplies from eastern Europe. One of the most widely used is the AK47 or Kalashnikov assault rifle. Another weapon much in demand is the 7.65-mm Vzor 61, commonly known as the Scorpion, from Czechoslovakia. This weapon is a machine pistol for it can give fully automatic fire of over 800 rounds a second but is little longer than an automatic pistol. Since it is small and hence easily concealable and as it is supplied with a silencer, it makes an ideal 'secret' weapon. Larger and far more devastating in the hands of trained terrorists are rocket launchers such as the Russian RPG-2, the RPG 7V and the RPG 7D. They deliver a grenade which can be extremely effective as an anti-tank, anti-aircraft or as a demolition weapon.

The supplying of weapons to terrorists or underground units has become a full-time business and the smuggling of firearms a remunerative trade. This gun-running can be done with the aid of secret landings from small boats anchored out at sea or, as in several authenticated cases, with the privileged diplomatic bag.

In addition to having access to the sophisticated 'hardware', the modern terrorist has the skill and knowledge to create explosives, booby traps, time fuses and incendiary devices from a range of household and commercially available materials, which makes these weapons extremely difficult to control or trace.

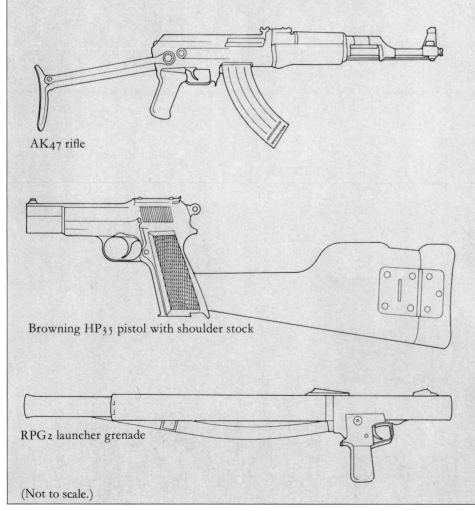

AK47 rifle

Browning HP35 pistol with shoulder stock

RPG2 launcher grenade

(Not to scale.)

adopted which consisted of a fibre liner with the inside suspension for the head attached and a separate steel cover which went over the fibre helmet.

The German First World War helmet was a very efficient defence and afforded greater protection to the back of the head and neck than either the French or British pattern. It has been modified slightly but, on the whole, has remained unchanged up to the present day. The Germans also introduced a form of body armour for their machine-gunners and snipers who might be in particularly exposed positions. The steel helmet was given a reinforcing plate to fit over the front whilst the body was protected by a number of very substantial, over-lapping, steel plates.

There were numerous experiments during the Second World War, particularly by the United States, on the possibility of giving their air crews some form of armour and many of the prototype helmets and pieces of armour are very similar to those worn during the Middle Ages. During the war in Korea (1950–52) body armour came into more general use and today most troops have some form of protective jacket which are nicknamed 'flak jackets'. Today modern materials such as plastics and ceramics are used with highly resist-ant steel in the construction of such clothing, which is highly

efficient and a Smith and Wesson Model 217, weighing only 9 pounds, will stop bullets up to .41 magnum, whilst lightweight ballistic shields can stop bullets up to .357 magnum. Special vests weighing only just over 5 pounds can stop .44 magnum 240 grain bullets – and there are few more powerful pistol bullets than this.

The First World War saw the large-scale use of grenades which had been abandoned by the troops from the mid-seventeenth century but which had made a return during the British campaigns in the Sudan. It was the Russo-Japanese War of 1904–05 that had seen the first modern use and from then on research and development into their design and use was intensified. Various models were produced which could be thrown or dis-charged from a specially adapted rifle. The Germans favoured the 'stick' type which had a 9/10 inch wooden handle containing the fuse which was ignited either before throwing or by the action of throw-ing. Today a wide range of these weapons are available both to troops and to the police.

The history of warfare in the twentieth century is sordid enough, yet in recent years new, even more sinister factors have been intro-duced. In the past the night gave hope to those who sought to move silently and unseen but today, with the use of various night sights,

even the cover of darkness has been removed. Some of these make use of infra-red radiation either given off by a body or projected and reflected from an object. These night sights may be in the form of a pair of binoculars (OB-24-A), as used by the French, or they may be an infra-red radiator (NSP2) as used by the Russians. Others use available light from stars, from the moon, or from the scattered light of buildings in the distance, and intensify this to a degree undreamed of a few years ago. With one of these sights such as the Tri-Lux L2A1, it is possible to pinpoint a target even in apparent total darkness.

Portable radar equipment is also used to give warning of the ap-proach of an unseen assailant. Units such as the Oliphant II give audible warning as well as the range of the target. The U.S. model AN/PPS5 gives visual indication of the move-ment of men up to a range of 5000 metres and of vehicles up to twice that distance.

One of the lessons to be learnt from the long story of arms and armour is that nobody wins in the end. When the armourer has the perfect defence then the weapon maker proves him wrong; when the weapon maker produces the ultimate weapon the 'defence' eventually shows that it is not – only people suffer in proving the point.

The Third World

The development of arms and armour in Europe follows a reasonably clear line of progression, but throughout the rest of the world the story is far less clear. In the West more and more resources and mechanical skills became available to the smiths and these technological advances were used to make better weapons and armour. In the rest of the world, the same resources were not to hand and it was left to each culture to fashion its weapons in accordance with its own particular life-style – the craftsmen used available materials to produce remarkably ingenious weapons.

When the Western nations started to explore and colonize, their technology made more of an impact on other civilizations than these did on the West. An exception might be the case of gunpowder, which originated from the East and which, ironically, was taken back by the Portuguese, the Dutch, and finally by the British.

After Classical times, the only Africa known to the West was that of fable and legend. In the nineteenth century, as the colonizers, missionaries, hunters and explorers moved further into the continent it gradually became clear that the range of weapons used by the various tribes was enormous. The craftsmen of Africa were, within the limits of their resources, highly skilled and their supply of weapons was generally limited to spears, knives and a few swords.

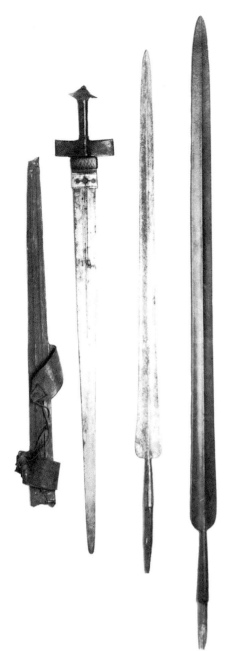

Spears were almost universal throughout the continent and there were great variations in size and shape. One of the best known was that used by the Masai of East Africa. It had a very short, central, wooden shaft, a long tapering ferrule and a blade which was like that of a sword, long and with the sides virtually parallel but swelling slightly just above the socket. The length of the blade was supposed to reflect the importance of the owner. The Masai also carried long-bladed swords with a very simple grip and virtually no guard for the hand.

Further south were the Zulus, who attracted the world's attention when they came into fierce conflict with the British. At Isandhlwana, in January 1879, the armies (known as *impis*) of Cetewayo overwhelmed and slaughtered many of the British 24th regiment of foot soldiers. Despite the Martini Henry rifles of the regular troops, the Zulu warriors swept in with their light *assegais* or throwing spears which were about 6 feet long with a 6-inch steel point. Each warrior carried a handful of these one of which was kept for hand-to-hand fighting as was a club of horn or wood, the *knobkerry*, which had a long, slim handle and a globular head. The shield, which was oval in shape, was of cowhide with the hair left on; it had a number of parallel

Above:
Left: Leather sheath and Sudanese *kaskara* with typical flat, broad cross-quillons.
Right: Masai spear blades and short wooden shafts which would have had long metal ferrules to complete the spear.

Left:
This carving from Benin (Nigeria) is of a Portuguese soldier of the 16th century. The rather crude detail of the musket seems to indicate that it is probably intended to represent a matchlock. The first firearms appeared in West Africa about this time but only became common at a later date.
British Museum, London.

Right:
West African carving of a man with a gun which is clearly a flintlock; the cock and frizzen would suggest that the original weapon copied was probably not earlier than the late 18th century.
Museum voor Land- en Volkenkunde.

slits, cut into it through which passed a strengthening stick which, along with some straps, served as a hand hold. Bows and arrows seem not to have been used much by the Zulus, probably because there was no suitably springy wood available for bow manufacture.

From the central part of Africa came a great variety of daggers, knives and swords. They are frequently crude in finish but may be very complex in design, often with numerous small blades attached at various parts to the main blade. Some were designed specifically as throwing weapons but in many cases the sheer complexity would seem to be self-defeating.

Further to the north, in the Sudan, were the Dervishes with whom the British army came into contact in the campaigns of the 1880s and 1890s. Among their weapons were a range of spears, including some from Somalia with an extremely large point, and also a sword with a straight, double-edged blade and a simple cross-guard with straight quillons and two long langets (bars) projecting down from the cross-guard to grip the throat of the scabbard. The grip was covered in leather and there was no pommel except for a flat, leather disc. This sword was known as the *kaskara* and is similar in shape to the crusading swords of the early Middle Ages. It was carried in brown leather sheaths which had a characteristic swelling shaped in the form of a spear point near the tip; the purpose and origin of this

Above:
In this 15th-century Timurid painting, the horses have padded coverings and the lances are stuck into the ground. The two riders have bows and arrows and wear similar armour to that of their horses. Painting from a copy of Khwaju Kermani's *Mathnawi*.
British Library, London.

Right:
Ceremonial axe from the Congo with the haft covered with copper sheet and the elaborate iron blade incorporating the images of fifty-eight heads.
Horniman Museum, London.

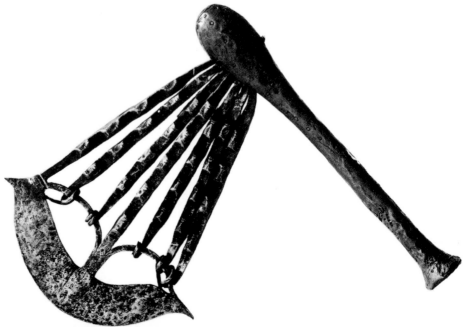

136

Above:
Jambiyah with hilt of rhino horn decorated with gold, and a sheath of gilded silver. It is probably 19th century and from North Africa.

Right:
This early Iranian 14th-century painting from a copy of Firdusi's Shah-nameh, shows the mounted warrior Bahram Gur, armed with a straight bladed sword as he attacks the lion. His bow is in a case at his side.
Spencer Collection, The New York Public Library, Astor, Lenox and Tilden Foundations.

shape is not at all clear, for it served no apparent purpose. A few were fitted into sheaths made from the skins of crocodiles with the sword going in through the open mouth. The scabbards were suspended from a short strap through which the arm was passed. Daggers were fairly crude, often with the blade bent almost at right angles and with a black, wooden X-shaped hilt.

The Sudanese were defended by a circular, elephant or rhinoceros hide shield, usually with a dome-shaped boss at the centre.

The Abyssinian tribesmen, with whom the British found themselves fighting in 1867, had a similar shield which was more often embellished with applied silver decoration. The characteristic Abyssinian sword was the *shotel* with a sickle-like blade and a simple horn grip, lacking any real guard.

In North Africa the Tuareg, a nomadic Arab people, carried a sword similar in general appearance to the *kaskara* but with a metal grip, a guard and a more recognizable pommel. From the same area came the arm dagger which was usually brass hilted and carried in a brass sheath fitted with a bracelet through which the arm was slipped.

Worn throughout much of the Middle East was the *jambiyah* which had a very wide blade with a sharp bend some few inches from the simple grip. The scabbard frequently emphasized this acute angle and was often covered with applied plates of embossed silver and wire or, if it was the property of a rich sheik, of gold.

As a result of their long association with Spain and their geographical closeness to Europe, the Arabs made a greater use of firearms than many other peoples. They seem to have preferred a style of musket long after it had been discarded in Europe. Flint-

137

WHIPS

Whips are not normally considered as weapons but they can be used as such. In America the quirt was commonly used by the cowboys and this was fashioned from flexible leather braided onto a short, wooden grip. It had two or four short lashes at one end and a wrist loop at the other. Sometimes the stock was hollow and filled with lead shot to give additional weight. Sometimes the ends of the horses' reins were braided together to make a simple form of quirt. The Australian stockman used a much longer whip which he could crack with great accuracy just behind the cattles' ears. In South Africa a broad, flat strap-like whip was known as the *sjambok* and was usually made from the hide of a rhinoceros or a hippopotamus.

In Europe a number of whips which concealed pistols were made, apparently for postillions on coaches. Most had a tubular stock which served as the barrel. Some of these pistols could only be fired when the lash was removed and the percussion cap placed in position (the trigger was a small button set in the stock). Other patterns could be fired with the lash still in position. A few of these whip pistols were made in India.

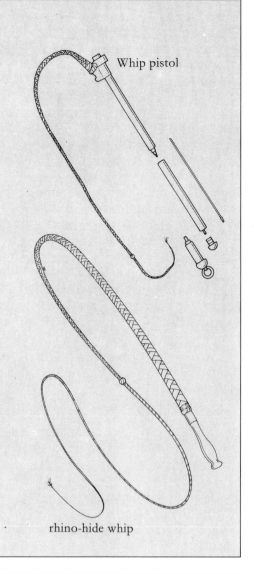

Whip pistol

rhino-hide whip

locks, from the seventeenth century onwards, had the steel and pan cover united to form an L-shaped frizzen. A variation of the flintlock, known as the snaphaunce, had the steel and pan cover separate. It was a style of design which did not last long in Europe but, for some reason, people of Northern Africa favoured this form of lock. Long after they had been discarded in Europe snaphaunce locks were still being made in Belgium, in centres such as Liège, for sale in the North African market. These were large and rather crudely finished but the numbers that survive clearly indicate that there was a considerable demand for them. The Arabs seem to have favoured the musket with a very long barrel and a butt which either had a deep cut curve to fit against the shoulder or one almost triangular in shape. The barrel on these *kabyles* was secured to the stock by bands, often of silver, and decoration was commonly applied to the stock.

Flintlock pistols of the Near East are also highly decorated with a variety of materials and styles: silver wire, beaten silver plates, coral, semi-precious stones and minerals, were all used in different ways by different countries. In Albania the rat-tailed miguelet pistol seemed to have been very popular. The miguelet was a special type of flintlock which had a different internal mechanism as well as a distinctive appearance: it had a frizzen with a square cut top and a squatter, more angular shaped cock. The stock on this rat-tailed pistol was, as the name implies, very thin and the butt tapered off to an almost sword-like pommel. In Turkey the pistols were frequently decorated with applied plates of beaten silver, silver wire, semi-precious stones; on the longer shoulder weapons, fringes of coloured material and tassels were not uncommon.

One form of firearm peculiar to Turkey and the surrounding area was what might be called the mini-blunderbuss for it was a scaled down version of the European model. The European blunderbuss had a barrel which flared out at the muzzle and fired, not a single

ball but a collection of perhaps a dozen small balls. The idea behind the design was that a wide muzzle would ensure that the load spread out and so increased the chances of a hit, although in fact the belling of the barrel had only a very minimal effect on the spread of the shot. In Europe the blunderbuss had been popular as a home defence weapon, and was also carried on mail coaches. Some Indian specimens often had extremely exaggerated bells to the muzzle as well as applied decoration on the stock and barrel. The Turkish examples were seldom more than between 18 and 24 inches long, the size indicating very clearly that they were intended to be used in one hand as a pistol.

The Cossacks of Russia produced a variant of the flintlock pistol with a slim wooden stock and a butt which curved down at quite an acute angle and terminated with a large ball pommel which was often made of ivory.

An edged weapon of the Balkans and Turkey was the *yataghan* which was a large, single-edged knife, usually with a slight curve to the blade, rather reminiscent of the Egyptian *khopesh* or the Greek *kopis*. The characteristic hilt had, in place of an ordinary pommel, two broad, round-angled wings at the end of the grip. The scabbard was often of metal or decorated with beaten sheets of metal.

The great range of spears and knives of Africa was probably only equalled by those of India, and the variety of edged weapons produced by that country would make a study in its own right.

Right:
These Greek soldiers fighting in the
War of Independence (1821–30), are
armed with the thin, metal stocked
flintlock pistols common in the Balkans.
The standing figure has a curved *kilij*
hanging from his wrist.

Below:
Typical Russian *kindjhal* or dagger
with the silver hilt and scabbard
decorated with niello work which gives
a black effect to contrast with the silver.

Swords are usually known simply as *talwars* although there are many variant forms. The commonest type of *talwar* had a single-edged blade which usually curved slightly backwards. The hilt was very simple in style with a large plate-like pommel, a slightly swelling metal grip, two very stubby quillons and on many a knuckle bow which curved up from the lower quillon to touch the disc pommel. Often the hilts were decorated with gold or silver and on many the pommel was chiselled as well. Most *talwars* had two short langets projecting down from the quillons and these gripped the neck of the wooden, leather or velvet-covered scabbard. It is of interest to note that these Indian weapons had grips which are normally a little too small for the hand of the European soldier.

Skill with the *talwar* or any other form of sword was greatly valued by the Indian warrior and their use was taught at *akharas* which were the equivalent of the European schools of fencing. These schools continued to teach until well into this century when they were still quite common. The shape of the hilt was, according to one writer, ideal for allowing a firm grip whilst still allowing manoeuvring, when even a small movement of the wrist could give a good slash. It was said that an expert Indian swordsman could stand with one knee against a tree and swing the sword backwards and forwards between him and the trunk without once touching it. The *talwars* were very sharp and contemporary accounts of the many Indian battles tell many harrowing stories of their terrible effects.

Whilst the majority of Indian swords had a curved blade there were some with a straight blade.

The *khanda* for example had a wide blade which was frequently strengthened by an extension rib along the back edge, although some were double-edged. The hilt differed from the usual *talwar* style in that it had a very broad knuckle bow and from the centre of the thickish disc pommel there sprang a large spike. This served a double purpose: it could be grasped by the left hand so turning the sword into a two-handed weapon; it could also be used as a form of dagger should the need arise. The *firangi* was very much like the *khanda* except that it lacked a strengthening rib and was double-edged. Often the blade was of European manufacture and its name means 'foreigner'. All these swords were normally carried in covered sheaths supported from a baldric across the shoulders.

From the Indo-Persian, Turkish areas came a much more sharply curved sword known as a *shamshir*. The hilts of these varied but many had only a small cross-guard and the pommel was at right angles to the grip, swelling into a bulbous knob which often took the form of an animal's head. Very similar is the *kilij* with a blade which widened towards the point. Occasionally the blade had such a pronounced

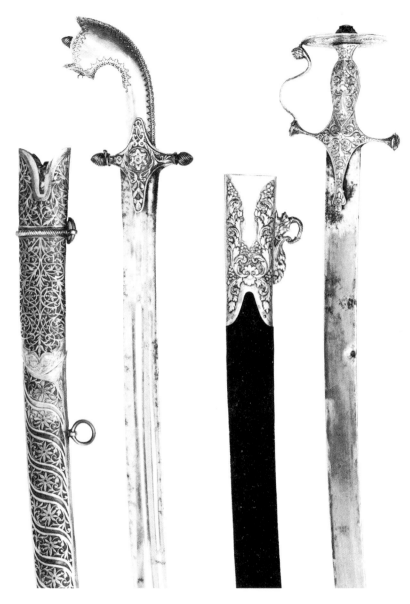

curve that either the back of the sheath was permanently split or else it had a spring-activated section which rose to allow the sword to be withdrawn; the angle was so sharp that the normal scabbard could not accept the sword.

The swords described above were the more common swords of India: many variations however were to be found throughout the length and breadth of the sub-continent. Some had double curves, others curved in one direction either to the left or to the right, and a few, apart from those mentioned above, had straight blades. The gauntlet sword, the *patá*, which was the weapon favoured by the Mahratta cavalry, consisted of a fairly broad blade which fitted into a metal half-gauntlet with a crossbar on the inside. The hand was slipped inside the gauntlet through a small chain, which crossed the

Above:
Left: This silver hilted sword is a strange mixture of east and west for in form it has both Indian and North African features but the quillons and scabbard are European in design. 19th century. $35\frac{1}{4}$ inches (89.5 cm).
Right: Although apparently an Indian *talwar*, this silver gilt sword carries London silver hallmarks for 1828.

Left:
Persian helmet, arm guard, sword and shield all decorated *en suite*. 19th century.

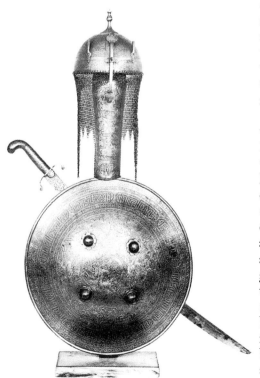

open end at the wrist. The central bar was gripped and the sword blade projected like an extension of the forearm. Often it was fitted with European blades because these were of a type and weight very suitable for the lance-like thrust that the weapon delivered. A smaller version of the *patá* was the *katar* which was a dagger of similar design and which was used as a punch dagger. Often the point of the blade was thickened in order to ensure a better chance of piercing mail.

The Indians made great use of daggers and a wide range of differ-ing styles were produced. In the north there was the *khyber* knife which, in its true form, was very large indeed – virtually a short sword. The cross-section of the blade was rather like a T with a pronounced back rib and it was very acutely pointed. One interest-ing and unusual feature about this weapon was that when it was sheathed, virtually the whole of the knife was covered with only the top inch or so of the hilt exposed.

Widespread over much of India and Persia was the *khanjar*. The rather thick blade usually had a slight double curve and a hilt which was of the 'pistol' type with just a small swelling at the pommel. These hilts are frequently of jade, ivory or other such rich materials. Often of very fine quality the dagger and sheath were decor-ated *en suite*.

Indian weaponsmiths achieved a remarkably high degree of skill in dealing with their materials and they delighted in decoration. They were also ingenious, producing weapons which had hidden blades; these were often long, thin bodkin-like spikes which were housed in the shaft of a club or even in another

Right:
Indian miniature from the 16th century in the *Chronicles of Jenghiz Khan in the years 1211–18*, showing Mongol soldiers in front of a Chinese fortress. A variety of weapons including catapult, match-lock, swords, cannon and bows and arrows are shown.
Imperial Library, Teheran.

Below:
Indian *khyber* knife with metal sheath. These weapons were produced in a great variety of sizes ranging up to those with blades 2 feet (61 cm) long.

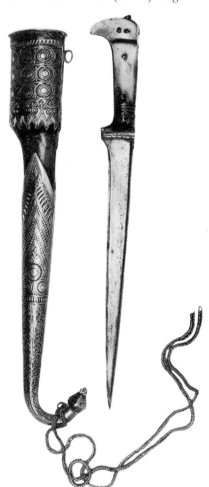

edged weapon. They also produced secret weapons of a more insidious type. The *bagh nakh* (tiger's claw) was a metal bar with either two holes or two attached rings at the end. Along the bar were fitted a number (usually four) of short, curved, hook-like blades. If the fingers were slipped through the holes the weapon could be con-concealed in a clenched fist and when the moment was right, a sweeping slash with the open hand would inflict a ghastly wound.

Maces and axes often formed part of the Indian armoury. Some were simple, others were complex with globular heads covered with spikes at the end of a straight shaft. Yet others had the head mounted at the end of a shaft fitted with a *khanda* hilt. A few Persian examples have the 'knob' in the form of a horned head.

Archery was an important part of Indian warfare and the main type of bow found in India, Persia and Turkey was the double recurved one. A few were of steel but the majority were composite in form with the bow staff built up of sinew, wood, horn and other materials. This, together with the shape, made it very strong and springy, and some remarkable feats of archery were achieved with these particular bows. A large number of arrowheads were used with different shapes for different purposes: broad heads for hunting, small ones for flight shooting and solid bodkin points for war.

Some groups developed weapons peculiar to their culture. The Sikhs had the *chakram* which is a thin, flattened steel quoit with a sharpened edge. These were made in a variety of sizes and when sent spinning towards an opponent they were an extremely unpleasant form of weapon.

Firearms in India were very much influenced by the strong contacts with Europe, which were often unwanted and sometimes forced on the sub-continent. Many of the weapons, which are still in use right up to this century, were matchlocks, because of the simplicity and therefore cheapness of their manufacture and maintenance. Known as the *torador* or *bunduk*,

the majority are very long and slim; the serpentine that holds the match let into the wood of the stock so that only the end is visible. Flint-lock and percussion weapons were also produced, and in more recent years small factories in the North-West territories make very good working copies of almost every type of modern cartridge weapons by hand.

Armour of India was, in many ways, similar to that of Europe. Mail was very popular and was worn as hauberks, as leggings, and fitted to helmets, or as coifs

Top:
18th- century Indian arm and hand armour. The steel plates are chiselled and decorated with silver and gilt. *Private collection.*

Above:
Indian armour comprising the four plates, *char aina*, shield (dahl) and two arm guards, all decorated *en suite.*

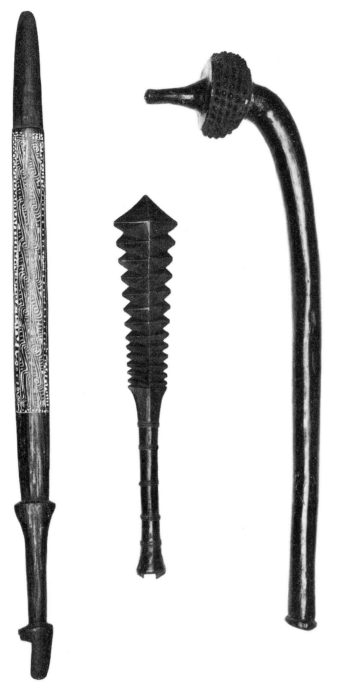

Left: Sword club from New Guinea, 30½ inches (77.5 cm).
Centre: Fijian dancing or ceremonial club.
Right: Fijian 'pineapple' club, 25½ inches (64.7 cm).

one at the back and one on each side. Protection for the arm was given by *dastana* which had a curved, metal plate to cover the forearms and a glove of mail for the hand.

Further east, the characteristic weapon in Malaya and in the islands of Indonesia was a particular form of short sword or long dagger, and this was the *kris*. The blade was produced by a process very similar to the European pattern-welding and the surface is usually rough with a dull, mottled appearance. Although many areas produced a weapon with its own peculiarities, most of the *kris* have certain common features. The blade, sometimes straight and sometimes sinuous, widened out at the top and so served as a hand guard rather like the quillons on a sword. The grip could be of metal, wood, bone or ivory and was often covered with patterns or figures. To accommodate the blade the sheath has a wide top section but the actual shape varied. In Malaya it was quite squarish, whereas in Bali it was much rounder and in Java it had upswept tips.

The peoples of South East Asia were familiar with metals but this knowledge did not extend across the Pacific. When the first explorers began to make their way across the Pacific ocean, they found innumerable islands the majority of which had no knowledge of metal. The indigenous inhabitants were therfore obliged to use the materials to hand. From coconuts they sometimes wove armour of plaited coconut fibre. In the Gilbert Islands the inhabitants fashioned *tebutje*, which were clubs to which were attached a number of sharks' teeth. Sharks' teeth were used for making short 'teeth' daggers as well as long, three bladed 'sword' clubs. Stone was also used and it is interesting to note that the axes produced in Polynesia were very similar in shape to those produced in the Stone Age. The craftsmen turned to naturally suitable materials, such as wood, from which they cut and fashioned clubs and on many islands this was a weapon of far greater importance than in almost any other culture. A great range of

similar to the European type (*kulah zirah*). The usual helmet consisted of a metal skull which was fairly shallow on the Indian ones and deeper on the Persian and Turkish types (*kulah khud*). From the brim was fitted a mail curtain and some protection to the face was given by a sliding nasal bar. Almost invariably the helmets are topped with a spike in addition to, or instead of, plume holders. Plate defences were also worn and these were usually in the form known as *char aina* – the four mirrors. They varied in shape and style but most consisted of four, slightly curved plates which fitted one at the front, shapes was developed and in Fiji there were clubs fashioned from naturally occurring roots and and trunks and those which represented hours and hours of laborious carving and scraping. Among the largest was the musket club so-called because of its general resemblance to the butt and projecting lock. Also from Fiji came the so-called pineapple club: this had a globular head set at an angle to the shaft which was cut into a square pattern – hence the name – and from the centre of which projected a vicious spike. The Marquesa island woodworkers produced one of the most unusual for as the top of the shaft flattened out into a cone shape it was carved to resemble a face.

Similar conditions prevailed further south in Australia and New Zealand. The weapons of Australian Aborigines were of wood or stone and they developed a form of weapon known and used by the Ancient Egyptians: the throwing stick. The weapon of the Aborigine culture is called the boomerang. Similar weapons are known to have been used in Africa, India and North America but the Australian version seems to be the only 'returning' type although in fact not all of them are designed to return. It should be remembered that if the boomerang hits its target it will, of course, fall and not return. The Australian variety was produced in a number of different styles and shapes but most are simply flat pieces of wood carefully shaped to produce just the right lift and turn. The ones that were not necessarily designed to return were the fighting ones, which were usually less curved. Clubs also featured in the Aborigine arsenal and they were usually very simple although occasionally decorated with some carving. One club was so designed as to double up as a shield: this was the *tamarang*, which was a piece of wood with a hand hold cut at the back and it could be used to parry or deliver a blow.

Aborigine spears were usually entirely of wood with perhaps a few barbs carved onto the shaft, whilst others had flint heads fitted.

Great use was made of spear throwers which were simply a system of artificially extending the length of the arm by means of flat, wooden sticks, with either an attached or carved hook. The spear thrower was held in the right hand and the spear placed so that the butt end engaged with the hook. When the arm was swung forward the thrower increased the power of the throw because the leverage was greater. The Aborigines also fashioned flint arrowheads in precisely the same way as Stone Age man.

In New Zealand the Maoris made great use of flat, paddle-shaped clubs. Bone specimens had a very sharp edge and were spatula in shape – these were *patu paraoa* – whilst a few were made of jade and were called *mere*. They would have proved to be extremely unpleasant if used to deliver a crushing blow at the nape of the neck. Another characteristic weapon of New Zealand was the *tewha-tewha*

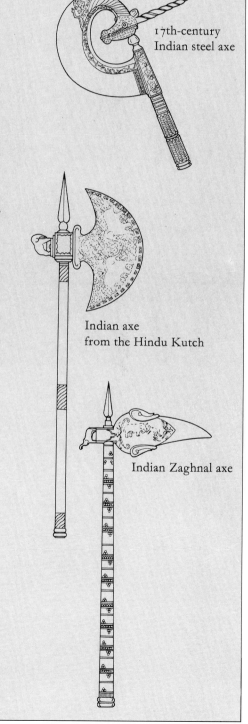

AXES
Although the axe had only a limited use in the West, it was a common weapon in the armouries of many Asiatic peoples until the late nineteenth century. In the sub-continent of India it was made with a variety of different shaped heads. Probably the most common axe was the *tabar* which had a crescent-shaped cutting edge, in some examples of which the tips of the blade were forked. The Nagas of north-east India used a thin, flat, almost triangular blade mounted on a long, wooden handle with characteristic 'tufts of of hair' decoration. From Nepal came the *ram-dao* which was a cross between a sword and an axe. It was used for sacrificial slaughter of goats and buffalo. The haft, which was sometimes of ebony, was fairly short, whereas the blade was long and broad with a distinct crescent shape near the tip. The shape of a human eye was cut into the steel blade near the tip. Further south, the Mahrattas used a thick, spike-like axe known as a crowbill. To the east in Borneo the *bilion* had a cutting head which could be mounted at right angles or parallel with the haft.

The Japanese used an axe with a long handle rather similar to the old Danish axe and this was named, appropriately, *O-No*.

17th-century Indian steel axe

Indian axe from the Hindu Kutch

Indian Zaghnal axe

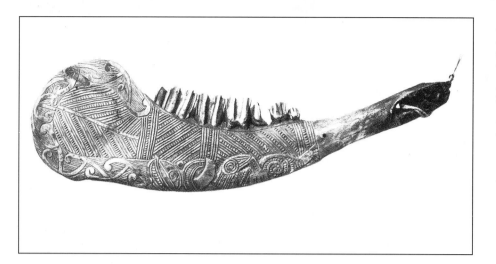

which was a form of club with a long, slightly tapered shaft, pointed at one end and with a flat, almost flag-like projection. A small bunch of feathers was attached to this blade which was intended to be flicked at an enemy to confuse him during the skilful form of fencing that was developed for these weapons.

In New Guinea was produced a club which was shaped very much like a broad-bladed sword, narrow in section and with a sword-like grip. It was used for slashing rather than for hitting, and was often decorated with quite complex line patterns cut into the wood.

A complete contrast to this non-metal technology was to be found further north in the Pacific. The Japanese acquired a mastery of metallurgy in certain fields that was never equalled anywhere in the world. The Japanese sword produced from the later Middle Ages onwards is probably the finest cutting weapon that has ever been made. The blade was the result of great care and ritual in its construction. The difficulty with all sword blades has always, from the Bronze Age onwards, been to produce a metal which was hard enough to take a good edge and retain it without making the blade too brittle. (Brittleness is a characteristic associated with hardness.) Many methods to overcome this obstacle were tried including

Mounted Japanese Samurai carefully wipes his blade. He wears only part of his armour.
British Museum, London.

the pattern-welding system used by the Viking swordsmiths. None, however, was quite as successful as that evolved by the skill and mastery of the Japanese swordsmiths.

Their solution was to create a kind of metal sandwich sword in which the centre part was of a softer metal than the outside. The outside metal, particularly at the cutting edge, was hardened so that it would take an edge and keep it. The manufacture was a long and complicated process and during his work the Japanese swordsmith was bound to observe certain rituals to ensure that the quality of the blade would come up to standard. The basic method of construction was to hammer and fold a block of steel many times and then a piece of high carbon – consequently very tough – steel was united with the softer block and hammered into one. When the blade had been shaped and checked, the outside was further hardened by being heated in a fire. The blade was covered with a thin coating of clay, charcoal and sand but the cutting edge was carefully cleared of this mixture whilst the rest was left for the clay to set. The sandwich of metal and clay was now placed in the furnace, cutting edge down, and heated up. When the metal showed the correct colour – a matter for the smith's decision – the blade was taken from the fire and dipped into warm water. The unprotected edge was cooled quickly and acquired an incredibly hard edge, whilst the clay-protected part cooled more slowly from a lower temperature and was, therefore, less likely to be brittle. If the blade of a Japanese sword is examined there is a wavy line a short distance in from the cutting edge, which is known as the *yakiba* and indicates the area cleared of clay. When cooled, the blade was cleaned up, sharpened and given its final, lasting polish. The basic shape for the Japanese blade altered hardly at all and had just a very slight curve.

The blade was fixed in the hilt in quite a different way from the Western method. Indian sword-smiths united the blade and hilt by means of a resinous glue compound, but the Japanese used a system which, on the face of it, seemed to be totally inadequate but was, in fact, perfectly satisfactory. The tang (the end section of the blade) which was some 4 to 5 inches in length, was drilled with a hole and then slotted inside the wooden grip. Through the grip and through the hole in the tang passed a small, wooden peg and, surprisingly enough, this very frail connection was perfectly adequate

and the sword could be used to deliver a very hard cut without significantly damaging the construction of the weapon.

The guard on these Japanese swords was very simple and the *tsuba* was little more than an oval or rectangular plate of metal which was fitted between the blade and the hilt. As with so many things the Japanese delighted in decoration and many *tsuba* are pierced, chiselled or inlaid with various materials. The grip on the Japanese sword was a wooden former covered with *same* which is a rough fish skin, ideal for getting a good grip. Over the *same* went a very elaborate and carefully designed binding of black braid, laced on in a zig-zag fashion. Under the binding were two fine small figures known as *menuki*.

When the sword had been assembled it could be tested and, with simple logic, the Japanese decided that really the best test for a fighting sword was to try it on a human body. Top quality swords

Above:
Clay figure of a Japanese warrior found in a burial mound, *c.* 500 AD. *Seattle Art Museum, Washington.*

Left:
Japanese helmet of the 16th century made in the classic shape of the period with a neck-guard of a smaller size than is found on many. The fan-shaped *kasajirushi* is a badge worn for much the same purpose as the crest on the helmets of European knights – easy recognition. *National Museum, Kyoto.*

Opposite top:
Japanese armour of the late 14th century superbly decorated with pierced and gilt panels. The large 'horns' on the helmet served a similar purpose to the crest on European helmets. The lacing to hold together the lacquered metal plates can be clearly seen. *Kasuga-Jinsha Shrine, Nara City.*

Opposite bottom:
Japanese armour sent by the Governor of Edo to James I of England in 1614. A saddle and a pair of stirrups completed the gift. *Tower of London Armouries.*

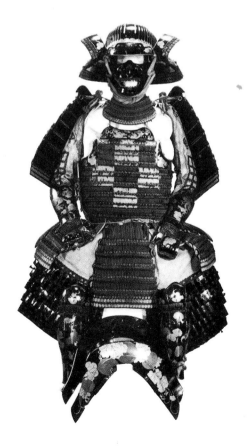

were often tested in this fashion, with a ritual cutting on a condemned criminal. This is known as *tameshi-giri*. The quality was assessed by the efficiency with which these cuts were made and the mere chopping of a hand was considered to be simple. The fact that the sword had passed its test was engraved onto the tang of the blade together with the name of the swordmaker. The blade itself was given a very high, durable polish which is one of the features of the Japanese swords and some examples have survived from the Middle Ages. Blades dated from the thirteenth and fourteenth centuries have a shine and a polish on them as bright as the day on which they were finished.

The warrior class of Japan was the Samurai who developed a code of life and culture which required them to have a pair of swords – a *daisho*. These were carried tucked

Above:
A Japanese suit of armour of the 16th century which clearly shows the lamellar construction of small plates and lacing. The face is protected by a plate fashioned into a grotesque mask.
Kozu collection, Kyoto.

into the waist sash in such a way that they were ready to be drawn instantly. The two swords making a *daisho* were the *katana*, which was a fairly long sword with a long hilt to accommodate the two-handed grip often used by the Japanese, and the *wakizashi*, which was a shorter sword. There was also a dagger known as a *tanto*. These swords were produced until well on into the nineteenth century when in 1876 the emperor forbad the wearing of them. Although a few makers continued to produce them the Japanese sword had virtually reached the end of its production line. Similar style blades were mounted on the end of shafts

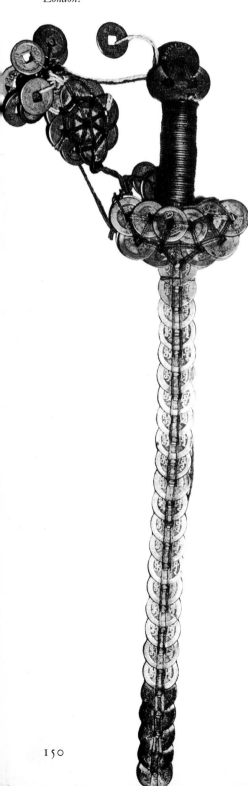

to produce the Japanese pole-arm known as a *naginata*.

The Japanese weaponsmith came into contact with the Portuguese and Dutch during the fifteenth century, but from the seventeenth century Japan was virtually cut off from western technology until the 1853–54 expedition by Commodore Perry who, in effect, broke the self-imposed blockade. The result was that the Japanese missed most of the intervening steps in the development of firearms, going straight from the matchlock to cartridges. The Japanese matchlock had a barrel which was usually large, octagonal and very heavy. Stocks were rather stubby and with a very short butt and the springs and fittings were almost invariably of brass. Since brass is not the best material for springs, one feature of the Japanese gun is that the movement of the cock has a very soggy feel to it.

The Japanese were keen archers and produced a bow which is unlike those from the West. The bow was gripped, not at the centre, but about one-third of the way up from the bottom of the 7-feet long shaft. The arrows were long and fitted with a great variety of different shaped heads and feathers.

Japan also developed a type of armour very different from that of the West. It consisted of a mixture of plate and mail, but was mostly of a lamellar construction with small metal plates that were usually lacquered and laced together. Often the armourer copied European armour in a Japanese style with solid plate breastplates. Japanese helmets were very different from those in the West and most had a skull made up of a large number of small plates, all fastened together to form a ridged bowl with a hole at the top through which to put the warrior's hair. At the front there was a small peak and the neck was guarded by a series of overlapping curved plates secured by laces so that they spread out protecting the whole of the back of the head, neck and shoulders. One other feature not seen in the West was the use of a personal flag which was fitted to the back of the armour and stood up on the end of a tall, thin pole.

Although comparatively speaking a near neighbour, China never developed the same skill in the manufacture of weapons and armour, and Chinese weapons were surprisingly clumsy or ineffective. Swords were either very large, two-handed, execution swords with a slightly curved blade, or rather ineffective pairs of swords carried in one scabbard. One weapon which appears to have been peculiar to the Chinese, although copied by the Japanese, was a repeating crossbow, *chu-ko-nu*, which could be mounted on a wall and operated by a lever to maintain a steady flow of bolts. Chinese armour seems to have been mostly of the 'jack' or brigandine type with small plates riveted to a garment.

When Columbus discovered the New World, he found the inhabitants armed with simple weapons, and the Spanish invaders were later able to overcome immense odds because of their superior

Bottom left:
Feathers were often used as a decoration on weapons and armour and this example of an Aztec featherwork shield shows a blue and purple *coyote*. *Museum für Völkerkunde, Vienna.*

Bottom right:
This water-colour of an Indian from Florida clearly shows the simple bow and quiver. On the left wrist the Indian wears a guard to protect his arm against the slap of the bow string. *Museum of Mankind, London.*

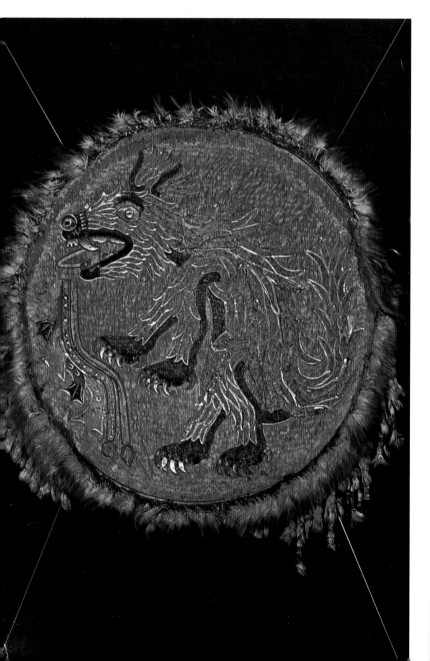

Above:
Selection of Red Indian tomahawks. Although the middle one is of the shape usually associated with this type of weapon, a range of different shaped blades was fitted. The top one is known as a spontoon pipe tomahawk and was used by Plains Indians. *Chandler-Pohrt Collection, Great Lakes Indian Museum, Cross Village, Michigan.*

Top right:
Shield of buffalo hide decorated with eagle feathers and hair, and belonging to Bull Lodge, a holy man and warrior of the Gros Ventre tribe of Montana, U.S.A. It dates from *c.* 1850 and is 19½ inches (49.5 cm) in diameter and approximately ⅜ inch (1 cm) thick. *Chandler-Pohrt Collection, Great Lakes Indian Museum, Cross Village, Michigan.*

armaments. The Red Indians learned fast and when they acquired horses they became some of the finest light cavalry in the world. They had various weapons including bows and arrows with which they were highly skilled, spears, and a club known as *I Wata-Jinga* with a stone head which was often enclosed in a rawhide bag and fitted to a long, thin shaft. The *tomahawk* was a popular weapon and consisted of an axehead of varying shape fitted to a stout wooden handle.

The *bolas* was a weapon that was used by both the Indians in South America and the Eskimos in the North. Two ball weights were secured to a thong one at each end, with a smaller one fixed to the centre. The centre ball was held in the hand and whirled around the head until the weights were moving at a high enough velocity, at which point the bolas was released. It spun through the air until it hit its target when the momentum of the

balls caused them to swing round and tie the thong round the target.

Today as a result of modern media and transport, few areas of the world are isolated and in most places the traditional weapons are no longer considered sufficiently powerful, efficient or lethal. Except where there are government restrictions there are few places where the hunter does not use a small calibre, high powered rifle, or the soldier a modern automatic weapon.

The industrialized nations of the West have brought about a worldwide uniformity in weapon technology. Where their technology has impinged on that of Third World countries it has in many cases destroyed the whole fabric of their culture and made their indigenous weapons redundant. The 'old' weapons are becoming scarcer and scarcer as the modern world no longer scorns them as 'primitive', but values them as objects of historical interest.

Bibliography

Robert Abell, *Classic Bowie Knives* (New York, 1967)
William Albaugh, *Confederate Edged Weapons* (New York, 1960)
L. J. Anderson, *Japanese Armour* (London, 1968)
John R. Angolia, *Daggers, Bayonets & Fighting Knives of Hitler's Germany* (California, 1971)
John R. Angolia, *Swords of Hitler's 3rd Reich* (Southend, 1969)
Philip Annis, *Naval Swords* (London, 1970)
James P. Atwood, *The Daggers & Edged Weapons of Hitler's Germany* (Berlin, 1965)
Howard L. Blackmore, *Arms and Armour* (London, 1965)
Howard L. Blackmore, *Hunting Weapons* (London, 1971)
Claude Blair, *European & American Arms 1100–1850* (London, 1962)
Claude Blair, *European Armour* (London, 1972)
William Carman, *Headdress of the British Army: Cavalry* (London, 1968)
William Carman, *Headdress of the British Army: Yeomanry* (London, 1970)
Jack Coggins, *Arms and Equipment of the Civil War* (New York, 1962)
M. H. Cole, *Collection of U.S. Military Knives 1861–1968* (Alabama, 1968)
H. R. Davidson, *The Sword in Anglo-Saxon England* (1962)
Arthur Dufty, *European Armour in the Tower of London* (London, 1968)
Arthur Dufty, *European Swords & Daggers* (London, 1974)
Charles Ffoulkes, *The Armourer and his Craft*, Reprint (New York, 1967)
Inami Hakusi, *Nippon-To* (Tokyo, 1948)
T. M. Hamilton, *Native American Bows* (Pennsylvania, 1972)
Ernest G. Heath, *The Grey Goose Wing* (New York, 1972)
James Hicks, *French Military Weapons* (Connecticut, 1964)
Gordon Hughes, *Primer of Military Knives* (Brighton, 1973)
Sakakibara Kozan, *The Manufacture of Armour & Helmets in 16th century Japan* (London, 1963)
Francis Lord, *Civil War Collectors Encyclopaedia* (Harrisburg, 1965)
Otis Mason, *North American Bows, Arrows and Quivers* (New York, 1972)
R. Ewart Oakeshott, *The Archaeology of Weapons* (London, 1960)
R. Ewart Oakeshott, *The Sword in the Age of Chivalry* (London, 1964)
Harold L. Peterson, *American Indian Tomahawks* (U.S.A., 1965)
Harold L. Peterson, *The American Sword* (U.S.A., 1965)
Harold L. Peterson, *Arms and Armour in Colonial America* (1956)
Harold L. Peterson, *Daggers & Fighting Knives of The Western World* (London, 1968)
Robert Rankin, *Helmets & Headdress of the Imperial German Army 1870–1918* (Connecticut, 1965)
Philip Rawson, *The Indian Sword* (London, 1968)
Luciano Rebuffo, *Italian Armour* (Turin, 1959)
Gérard Regnier, *Infanterie Pickelhauben* (Paris, 1974)
Basil W. Robinson, *Arts of the Japanese Sword* (London, 1961)
H. Russell Robinson, *Oriental Armour* (London, 1967)
H. Russell Robinson, *The Armour of Imperial Rome* (London, 1976)
Brian Robson, *Swords of the British Army* (London, 1975)
Christian Henry Tavard, *Les Armes Blanches Modernes* (Paris, 1971)
Floyd Tubbs, *Stahlhelm* (U.S.A., 1971)
John Walter, *Sword & Bayonet Makers of Imperial Germany 1871–1918* (London, 1973)
John Walter, *The German Bayonet* (London, 1976)
G. R. Watson, *The Roman Soldier* (London, 1969)
G. Webster, *The Roman Army* (London, 1956)
Frederick Wilkinson, *Battle Dress* (London, 1970)
Frederick Wilkinson, *Edged Weapons* (London, 1970)
Frederick Wilkinson, *Swords & Daggers* (London, 1967)

Index